ANANSI
CHRISTIAN COUNSELLOR

THE BULLIES

Creative Ministry Resources Publishing
Email: creativeministry_music@gmail.com

Paperback ISBN: 978-976-96137-7-5
Hardback ISBN: ISBN 978-976-96137-6-8
Ebook ISBN: 978-976-96137-7-5

TABLE OF CONTENTS

TABLE OF CONTENTS

PREFACE

The popular Jamaican folklore charac-ter Anansi, known for his cunning and craftiness, has returned to the world center-stage as a spiritual mentor. With no less of his old craftiness, Anansi now teach-es with the wisest and most cunning meth-ods, how to deal with everyday life issues.

Anansi who is extremely rich from his old trickery and past antics, now deploys his wealth to help others.
Everyone marvels at Anansi and says, "His generosity exceeds his past infamy!"

Anansi has adopted a theme song, FIFTY DOLLAR NOTE, to which he commits and lives. It is the prayer of his life to God. Everyone who has been to Anansi would hear this song playing multiple times. They would often hear him say, "Anansi, Anansi, Anansi, this is me, I live this song."

In this series, Anansi Christian Counselor has a powerful message for children who are being bullied, and a powerful message for bullies.

FIFTY DOLLAR NOTE

I want to have Your Spirit
I want to have Your mind
I want to have Your seal
Then use me O Lord
Send me where you want to
To touch the hearts of man
To be spent for Your people
This is what I want

Spend me like the fifty dollar note
Let me be the one You use the most
A currency of heaven
To be spent down here on earth
To be tendered for Your people
Use me Lord

BOOK ONE

VERBAL BULLYING

CHAPTERS IN BOOK 1

JOHN'S DILEMMA

JOHN VISITS ANANSI

ANANSI COUNSELS JOHN

JOHN'S DILEMMA

"I am not going back," John said to himself. He was sitting under a tree behind his house crying uncontrollably. "I am not going back to school. Nobody likes me at school."
John reached up and felt his nose. "Why did God have to give me such a big nose?" he said to himself sobbing. "Why must He be so harsh to me?"
"The children will not stop teasing me about my big nose." John could not restrain himself. Tears fell from his hurting and pitiful eyes. He felt so bad about it. He felt so very bad about himself.

John could hear his mother calling him, "John, John! Where are you? John, John! Where are you?" John did not answer his mother. He did not want her to know what he was going through. He loved his mother but she could not help him. "She will only make a bad situation worse," he whimpered. "She will come to my school and embarrass me."

He remembered the time he was at the other school. He had told his mother, "The children are teasing me at school. I hate my nose. I don't want to go back to school."
"You have to go, son," his mother had asserted while seeing John off to school.
After John had left, his mother sat for a moment feeling angry. She then got dressed and stormed into his school.
She did nothing less than go there to defend her son. On that day she was wearing her market clothes with her dirty apron. She sold ground produce in the market and she had simply dressed for work. Her shoes were torn and dirty.

She did not follow standard protocol. She ignored the security guard in her anger. She simply barged into John's classroom while it was in session. The teacher was flustered.

Mother did not address the teacher or ask her for permission to speak. She simply took over the class and began addressing the other students. "Leave my child alone!" she shouted in an angry voice. "All of you; leave my child alone! His nose is big because mine is bigger. Look at it!" she said. There was pride in her voice; she was ignorantly boastful.

John still blushes to this very day and the intense heat returns to his cheek every time he remembers what she did at school that day.

She took her hand and opened her nose as if mimicking an enraged bull to demonstrate.

"If John's nose is big," she said, almost singing this time, as if proud of herself, "mine is bigger. My name is Mamma Big Nose, and I am proud of it!"

The laughter was embarrassing. It distracted the entire school.

The teacher stopped her at that point and asked her to leave. By that time the security guard was at the door so she had no choice.

The children roared with laughter.

John's cheeks got intensely hot again.

"I do not know who was, rather, is, more embarrassed about it," he said to himself, "Mamma or me."

My heart felt sad to see the security guard escort her out of the classroom, and practically drag her through the gate but I was glad to see her leave. Everyone in the school started to call me, "Mamma Big Nose" after that. It makes me feel a thousand times worse about my nose.

John could hear their chants in his head, "Big nose, big nose! Mamma big nose, Mamma big nose! Mamma boy, big nose, Mamma big nose!" He grunted as their squeals of laughter flooded his mind. "Even the children who did not tease me before joined in. They all started teasing me now."

There was one little girl, just one, who had sympathy on him. She always defended him but that was not enough. That too made him feel bad.

"I had to leave and go to a different school," John said to himself.

"The teasing was very bad. I was happy when the principal asked my mother to move me because of her bad behavior. She had earned the title of the most infamous and notorious parent at the school," he chuckled through his tears.

"I am at a new school now but the situation is the same. It seems that my nose just keeps picking out people. At least, people keep picking out my nose. I am not returning to this school. I am not going back to any school!" John said to himself. He was resolved about it, "I am not going back to school."

"John, John! Where are you?" John could hear his mother's voice getting closer. He knew he should never disrespect his mother, even though she made him feel so bad sometimes. He still had to love and honor her. This is exactly what his Children Church teacher told him.

John smiled as he thought about his teacher. The song 'Love Will Pick You Out' echoed in his heart:

> THERE IS SOMEONE WHO NEEDS YOU
> YOU ARE A PERFECT STAR
> LOVE WILL PICK YOU OUT ON THE GLOBE
> AMONG THE MILLIONS WITH YOU IT FINDS YOUR SOUL
> IT WILL AMAZE YOU HOW STRAIGHT IT GOES
> AND ANYWHERE YOU ARE AROUND THE WORLD
> LOVE WILL PICK YOU OUT

The teacher made him feel very good about himself in spite of everything. Everybody treated him differently at children church. They told him he was special.

John got up and went to the pipe to wash his face. Thoughts of children church had lifted his spirits and motivated him. He then went to meet his mother.

"Where were you?" his mother asked him, with worry and concern in her voice.

"I was behind the house," John said.

His mother could sense that something was really wrong with John but she was afraid to ask him. She could see his eyes were red and she knew he was crying. She did not ask him about it anymore, though. She remembered what she had done at his other school and how the children laughed at her and teased John afterwards. She felt she would only make the situation worse.

John's mother was not educated, and she wasn't very sure about herself either. She had a very hard childhood. She loved God, and she would pray every day about the situation. Praying made her feel so much better. She believes that every time you feel bad about something and don't know what to do, you should pray. Praying certainly helps you feel better and teaches you how to make better decisions.

"I was calling you to come for your dinner," Mother said to John.

John did not feel like eating anything at the moment. His heart was full and it filled his stomach. Sadly, he could not tell his mother. She worked so hard to provide as a single mother, and she would make such a fuss about it. John did not know his father. He lived with his mother alone from birth. This made him feel worse about himself, unprotected, and insecure. It was not his fault but he did not know it.

John was surprised at the table when his mother turned to him and said lovingly, "John, I am going to take you to Anansi."

"Wow! Anansi, yes!" John said, almost screaming the words in excitement. The theme song of Anansi began playing in his head immediately:

> I WANT TO HAVE YOUR SPIRIT
> I WANT TO HAVE YOUR MIND
> I WANT TO HAVE YOUR SEAL

THEN USE ME O LORD
SEND ME WHERE YOU WANT TO
TO TOUCH THE HEARTS OF MAN
TO BE SPENT FOR YOUR PEOPLE
THIS IS WHAT I WANT

SPEND ME LIKE THE FIFTY DOLLAR NOTE
LET ME BE THE ONE YOU USE THE MOST
A CURRENCY OF HEAVEN
TO BE SPENT DOWN HERE ON EARTH
TO BE TENDERED FOR YOUR PEOPLE
USE ME LORD

"Mother knew everything I have been going through. But it appears that she was just planning a better solution all this time," John thought. He felt a new respect for her as he could see the control she must have discovered and the maturity she had gained in her leadership.

Everybody knew Anansi was wise, very wise. He helped many people who were going through problems. Both adults and children went to Anansi for advice and help.

The talk in the town was that Anansi had the wisdom of God Himself. They say it was as if God talked to Anansi in person and gave him the right and precise words to counsel people.

"How are you going to do that Mamma?" John asked. "Anansi does not have the time. Everybody goes to him; much more important people than us. And even if he had the time, my big nose would frighten him!"

The words came out before John realized what he was saying. He wished he could take them back. Mother blushed and said, "Do not worry about that son. Anansi is having special sessions this week for children who are being bullied by other children. In addition to this, I have discussed the situation with my pastors. They have already arranged everything. We go tomorrow! You do not need to go to school tomorrow."

"As if I intended to," John thought.
John saw his mother smile slightly and he knew she really wanted to help him.
"Thank you very much mother," he said, reaching over and hugging her. He then planted a kiss on her cheeks.

John, like everyone else in the village, had faith in Anansi. He knew that if no one else could help, Anansi would help him.
"You know mother," John responded. "I have heard the stories everyone tells in the village about Anansi. Anansi is a local folk legend."
"The stories are all true, John. Anansi was very cunning before he got saved. In the past, Anansi would easily outsmart everyone else. They say, he became rich just using his head. He always won.
Today, Anansi is still extremely rich, dirt rich, but we love him for it. He has been so generous since he became a Christian, we are all happy he is rich. It is as if if his wealth belongs to us all. He lives his favorite song."

> SPEND ME LIKE THE FIFTY DOLLAR NOTE
> LET ME BE THE ONE YOU USE THE MOST
> A CURRENCY OF HEAVEN
> TO BE SPENT DOWN HERE ON EARTH
> TO BE TENDERED FOR YOUR PEOPLE
> USE ME LORD

"They say the time Anansi got saved was the only time he ever lost," John said.
"Oh yes, it is true," his mother said. "I was in church that day."
Mother began to tell the story John had heard so many times before.

Anansi tried to trick the preacher one day.
"Preacher I want to give a big offering to the church. A very big offering, but I must get to hold it."
He had a wry smile on his face.
Anansi thought of disappearing with the offering us-

ing this agreement as his defense.

The preacher thought about it for a short while.

"I will allow you to do this Anansi...." he paused as if pondering, "... but only if you allow me to tell you what offering to give."

"That is no problem at all," Anansi said. Then smiling to himself he whispered, "I am going to hold it anyway."

In his mind's eye, Anansi saw the preacher giving him the duty to collect the offering. He saw himself disappear with everything, his money and everyone else's. He could imagine the entire church screaming at him as he ran, some running after him.

"Stealing the show indeed!" Anansi said to himself. " I already have my defense. The preacher has agreed to my terms."

Looking at the preacher, Anansi said silently, "Rather your problem, Preacher. You are about to find out that whatever comes into Anansi's hand, stays in Anansi's hand."

Anansi smiled again at the preacher deceitfully.

"Come to church early tonight," the preacher said.

Anansi departed the preacher's presence dancing and chanting:

Come to church early
And I am gonna show
Before the preacher knows it
I will steal the show!

"Literally," he thought, laughing.

Anansi always made the sacrifice and special effort when he thought he was going to win. He will certainly be there early–extra early.

Anansi dressed up and was off to church. He was at the door before church started. He was the first to arrive.

Anansi thought, "The preacher will certainly tell me how much money to give as an offering, then he will allow me to usher and collect the offering tonight."

The preacher was ready for him when he

turned up that night. He shook Anansi's hand and said, "Hello Anansi. I am glad you could make it."
"I would not miss this for anything," Anansi replied, a little too eagerly.
"Before I tell you what offering to give, you must learn this offering scripture by heart.
This is your scripture, John 3:16. Memorize it. For God so love the world that He gave..."
Anansi turned to the text. He sat down and began memorizing the passage.
He continued repeating the passage under his breath: "For God so loved the world, He gave His only begotten Son, that whoever believes in Him should not perish but have everlasting life.
For God so loved the world, He gave His only begotten Son, that whoever believes in Him should not perish but have everlasting life."
"Yes!" Anansi said to himself when he thought he had it.
He had studied and memorized this scripture in a very short time.
Anansi had a very sharp mind, and he was very smart. Unfortunately, he used it to be cunning and deceptive.
"I cannot afford to lose or to give the preacher an advantage over me. One of my secrets of success is to take the time to study and learn my opponent's craft.
I always analyze the situation in every possible way to devise a strategy to stay ahead and to win. I will analyze this scripture also."
The preacher did not give Anansi the chance to use his head, and to pull off his scheme. He had a plan.

The service started.
The preacher had a very short worship service. It was strategic.

I GET LOST IN WORSHIP
I FOLLOW YOU WITH PRAISE
WANT TO COME INTO YOUR GARDEN

To see You face to face
We could talk and walk together
Or we could just commune
Want to soak you up like Moses
Lead me unto You

Holy Spirit Lead the way
Come and guide my heart
I will follow You with praise
Take me where You are
Let the heavens now awake
As I press into You Lord
Holy Spirit Lead the way
Take me where You are

After worship, the preacher said to the congregation, "We are changing the order tonight. We will collect the offering later." He then began preaching his sermon

"Oh no!" Anansi agonized, "I have to sit through the sermon before I am given the chance to pull off my scheme. It has been a long time since I have been to church. I did not bargain for this"

"I will be speaking to you today from the book of John, the third chapter and the sixteenth verse; John 3:16."

"That is the same scripture he gave me to memorize," Anansi said, his ears perking.

The preacher continued, "I want to tell you about Jesus. He is the Son of God. We were all born in sin. Everybody sinned and was condemned to hell. Jesus came from heaven to die for our sins.

He is the precious Son whom God loved dearly, but God sent Him to die for us so we do not have to go to hell.

Jesus was tempted like a normal man but He never ever sinned. He never lied, or deceived, or cheated, or stole."

The preacher paused strategically to let the point take effect.

Anansi felt self-conscious. "Why did he have to

pause so long when he said cheat and steal? Why is everyone looking at me?" he mumbled under his breath. He was sure everyone was looking at him because the words had exposed his heart in a way he had never seen himself before.

Anansi held his head straight, looking at the preacher, secretly conscious and convicted. He then said to himself, "For God so loved the world, that He gave His only begotten Son, that whoever believes in Him ...this Jesus concept is bigger than I am. My heart cannot ignore it. I feel so dirty."

The preacher talked for a little while more, then he was finished. Anansi was brought back to reality.

The preacher then said, "We will collect the offering now."

"This is the time I have been waiting on, but I do not have the heart for it anymore," Anansi lamented. "How can I steal from this God of love who gave His Son for me? I just hope the preacher will ask for something small or at least reasonable. This is going to be a total loss for me. How can I steal it back from the church?"

The preacher was resolute. He turned to the congregation and said, "The only offering I am going to ask for tonight is the most precious gift anyone of you can ever give."

Anansi's heart fell. "Preacher had me targeted. He is going to strip me of everything now, or at least of something big and valuable. Preacher hooked me with the message, now he is ready to scale me."

The preacher continued, "All that I am going to ask you for is that you give your life to the Lord Jesus Christ. When you give your life to Jesus, you get to hold it, and to keep it. Jesus only makes it richer and better."

Anansi got up and gave his life to Jesus that night. He was among the first respondents to the altar. The music played in the background:

HE DIED ON THE CROSS
TODAY IS THE DAY
IF YOU HEAR HIS VOICE
DO NOT HARDEN YOUR HEART
HE'S KNOCKING RIGHT NOW
DON'T TURN HIM AWAY
YOU DON'T HAVE TO BE LOST
HE DIED ON THE CROSS

"Jesus has me pinned down," he thought. "Preacher lets me off the hook with the money, but I fell into his net."
Anansi secretly licked his lips, "Richer and better huh!
Preachers are not like me. They are not supposed to tell lies. Richer and better huh!"

It was the big news in the community the next morning. It was so significant, the leading newspapers carried it, "Anansi is a Christian. Jesus reached out to another thief from the cross. Even the deceiver can be delivered when he meets the Saviour."
The community was in a buzz. It was a major event. Everybody was talking.
"Impossible," one man said. "He will show his colors soon. He will not last long!"
Another person who had lost a bet to Anansi commented, "Nobody believes him. This is just one of his tricks. He is too crafty."
"Let us give him one week," they agreed.
Anansi, however, was not to be distracted. He began studying his Bible and praying, day and night. "I must master this Christian faith," he committed to himself. "Nothing is ever going to beat me."
His motive was wrong but his approach was perfect.
"Wow!" Anansi exclaimed, reading his Bible. "The real wisdom is in here! All wisdom comes from God. This is the true wisdom."

Not long after Anansi felt compelled to teach about God. He used his intelligence to find creative ways of illustrating the truth of the scriptures. He became so wise and good that even the spiritual leaders came to consult with him. Today Anansi is a double legend for opposite reasons.

1. *GOD IS ABLE TO MAKE ALL THINGS NEW; THERE IS NO SITUATION TOO HARD FOR HIM – NOT SAUL'S WHO BECAME THE APOSTLE PAUL, NOT ANANSI'S, NOT YOURS.*
2. *WHEN YOU BELIEVE YOU ARE TOO FAR GONE, OPEN UP TO GOD, HE HAS GONE FURTHER SO HE CAN BRING YOU BACK.*
3. *YOUR PRESENT DOES NOT DICTATE YOUR FUTURE, YOUR PRESENCE OF MIND AND HIS PRESENCE DOES!*

JOHN VISITS ANANSI

"**I** am so very happy to be able to meet with Anansi alone. I am extremely proud to receive his counsel." John said.

He then began daydreaming of meeting with Anansi. "If when I arrive at Anansi, he treats me well, it does not matter who treats me badly after that. Anansi has such a great reputation, I will believe anything he tells me. If he says my big nose is small, it is small."

Such was the reputation and impact of this Anansi character.

"Based on what I hear, Anansi never treats anybody poorly...well, since the day he got saved anyway." John then paused to think about his nose. He fumbled and looked uncertain, "Perhaps my big nose will frighten him!"

The day passed with John still daydreaming of his meeting with Anansi. The night went by slowly for him. He woke up about four times and looked outside to see if morning had arrived. John could hardly wait. He wanted to wake up the sunrise. When morning finally came, John went and knocked on his mother's bedroom door.

"Mamma, see, it is morning now. Come let us go to Anansi."

"Not yet, my son," His mother replied yawning. "Our appointment is at ten o' clock. You will have to eat breakfast first and then do your chores. Mamma wants you to grow right, hardworking and intelligent. You will see Anansi soon."

John passed the time doing his chores. He was very excited, laughing and talking to himself in a congratulatory tone all the time.

He broke out singing, "Yes! Yes! I am going to Anansi; I am going to Anansi, yes, yes." He then

screamed.
"This feeling is overwhelming. The only way to get rid of this is for Mamma to let us go...right now!"

John was ready a full hour before his mother was. He sat under a tree and fantasized about his meeting as he waited.
"What is that story Mamma told me about Anansi? She was so depressed. She needed counseling herself when Papa left and never came back. Anansi gave her a fresh start at that time."
She would mimic the voice of Anansi as she said: 'Mrs. Grace, the only person you cannot live without is Jesus. Joseph was in a bind when his brothers sold him into Egypt. Joseph maintained his faith and kept working hard with a heart of excellence despite the hurts and emotional crush that he was experiencing. It was painful beyond feeling. Even when things seemed to be going down as Joseph's status declined from a slave to a prisoner, he kept working with excellence, looking beyond his situation to the God he served. He would do every task as if he was doing it for the God of His father's Jacob, Isaac, and Abraham.'
Anansi looked directly at me and said, 'Look at where it took him in the end. God exalted him because he never gave up or surrendered to his circumstances.'"
"I know the story of Mamma and Anansi by heart," John reflected. "Mamma tells it all the time."
Just then, John heard the voice of his mother coming to him from inside the house, "John! Where are you, John? We are ready to go now!"
He jumped up from his daydream. He set off running. He reached his mother in a flash, and took her hand proudly.
He thought, "I am very proud to hold mamma's hand today. I am not ashamed of what she did anymore. Today, I am going to be entertained in the luxurious home of Anansi."
In truth, Anansi always takes care of the peo-

ple who come to him very well.

"You know John," his mother said. "There are some people who still talk and say, Anansi tricked people so much in the past that he feels obligated to give back everything now. In secret, they call Anansi, Zacchaeus the tax collector."

"Why do they do this mother?" John asked very curiously. "It must be something bad because they whisper when they say this about him."

"Zacchaeus was a thief who gave back a half of his wealth to those he robbed when he met Jesus. He became very generous," Mother explained.

John and his mother arrived at the bus stop a few minutes later. They could see the bus coming down the road. It was on time that morning and they got on board.

After a few minutes, John said to his mother, "Mother, this ride is taking too long. Are we there yet?"

"Have patience son," his mother said, hugging him. The people in the bus were speaking and the radio was playing a popular song that John liked very much: Love Will Pick You Out.

John continued daydreaming about his meeting. All the noise and activity in the bus got lost in his excitement and anticipation.

After a while, the bus stopped in the prestigious part of town where Anansi lived.

The words of the bus driver pierced the armor of John's thoughts, "Nancy Stop!"

John jumped, then quickly came alive. "Let us go, mother," he said.

John and his mother stepped off the bus.

As they walked, John asked, "What time is it, mother?"

"It is 9:30 son," his mother responded. "Did you notice, Anansi is so popular, they do not even call the street by its real name; they just said, 'Nancy stop!'"

ANANSI COUNSELS JOHN

John and his mother stepped off the bus and walked excitedly to the house of Anansi.
It was monumental, a distinguishing landmark in this rich neighborhood. John remembered the moment he met with Anansi. The place was very nice and posh. Anansi's workers were very courteous and extremely pleasant.

John and his mother arrived for the appointment twenty minutes early. The courteous servants made them sit in a very large and beautiful room, with air conditioning and a television. The servants served them drinks and a snack as they waited.

"I would return any day, just for this exceptional treatment," John thought.

What John remembered most; what was most memorable to him was his first meeting with Anansi.

Anansi came into the room to the sound of his favorite song, Fifty Dollar Note. It is said that this song motivated him and kept him inspired.

> A currency don't dictate
> How it should be used
> The one who should receive it
> Or what it is used to do
> It does not tell its owner
> Where it wants to go
> And even so my Master
> I submit myself to You
>
> Spend me like the fifty dollar note
> Let me be the one You use the most
> A currency of heaven
> To be spent down here on earth

To be tendered by the people
Use me Lord

"This is your best friend Anansiiiiiii!" he said, almost singing as he looked directly at John and his mother. He held the "I" down in Anansi until you could feel him.

"This is very warm and nice," John thought. "It is real, it is roots, it is personal."

Anansi knew well how to deal with people, everyone alike. He could communicate with kings or presidents and yet he had the right style and approach for the ordinary man, and even for a child.

"Hello John!" he said, in his deep yet silky voice. John was amazed, the famous Anansi had called him by his real name.

He was pleasantly surprised, "No one ever does that, at least, not for a long time now," he thought. "The children calls me Big Nose and teacher call Johnny Cake. They think it is funny, but I never get the joke. Not even a small part of it. I would get the sting of it only, and it would pain me for days, every day."

"John, I am glad you could make it. I was expecting you," Anansi said. "You are such a handsome young man. I am really happy you could make it." He spoke in perfect English, then as if for emphasis, he repeated in patois, "Mi glad yuh cudda cum."

The warm smile that accompanied his words made John believe that this man was really genuine. John was knocked off his feet immediately. This important man made him feel very special. "As if he and I were equals," John thought.

"Am I the one you are calling handsome Sir?" John said. "Do not tell me a lie. Everyone calls me Big Nose.

The real truth is, Mr. Anansi, I am here to you because the children at school are teasing me that I am ugly, and I am very frustrated by it!"

Anansi placed a gentle hand on John's shoulder and sat him down in front of him on a soft and

comfortable seat. He looked into John's eyes and said, "They called me ugly too when I was young." "You!" John exclaimed, surprised. It was as if in his mind Anansi was the most perfect person he had ever seen. Anansi brought him back to reality right away. "How many limbs do I have?" he asked. Understanding entered John's eyes as he said, "Eight Sir!"
Anansi was silent for a short while. He wanted John to work it out for himself. He wanted to give John time for his imagination to run. He wanted John to have the time to visualize what it must have been for Anansi growing up being different. He wanted to give John time to put Anansi's anomaly into his own school's reality.
He could see John unconsciously drawing closer to him as if for the first time he could really connect. It was as if John wanted to help Anansi retroactively. It was also as if John was beginning to feel comfortable.

John was visibly more relaxed.
"I feel so connected to this important and accomplished person, almost as if we are equal. We both share our private pain in common."
Anansi said to John in patois, "But mi did wiser dan dem, mi boy," then he repeated in perfect English, "I was much wiser than them my son, John."
"Mi did wiser dan dem," he said again in patois. "They paid dearly for underestimating me. I am not proud of it now, but that is the reality"
"I have some things to tell you John," Anansi continued. "I wish I knew them then, I would never have tortured myself so much in the early days."
"Look in this mirror," Anansi said, handing John a mirror. "What do you see?"
"A very big and ugly nose, Sir," John said. "My nose is extremely big Sir!"
"Do you know God has a mirror?" Anansi said.
"When He sees you in His mirror, what do you think He sees?"
John was about to say, "He turns away His face."

But something inside him told him that was not true at all. He paused.
The silence continued for a few minutes. Anansi was humming a tune:
> "HOLY SPIRIT LEAD THE WAY
> COME AND GUIDE MY HEART"

Anansi chipped in under his breath as if trying to guide John's thinking. "Made in the image of God!" he said under his breath
John heard him and what he said came home strongly to him then. He had heard it many times before. "Made in the image of God," he repeated in his mind.
"Fearfully, wonderfully, marvelous…" Anansi said under his breath again and it hit home for John again. John remembered the Children Church lessons he was taught. "They always told me I was made in the image of God."
He could recall the text, Genesis 1:26-27.
"They told me, I was fearfully and wonderfully made and God considered His work on me, John, to be marvelous. What was that text again?" he asked himself. Then it came to him, Psalm 139:14.
"They told me in children church that God thinks about me as much as the sand of the sea. That was Psalms 139…? Yes Psalms139:17-18."
"What was that one about hair? God counted the number of the hairs on my head. That was Matthew10:30."
"When God looks at me He sees Himself" John ventured, looking up shyly, hoping he did not embarrass himself.
Anansi applauded. He looked at John approvingly and nodded. "He sees nothing else."
"That means nothing is wrong with me, Sir!" John said.
"Nuttin nuh wrang wid yuh!" Anansi said in patois; then he repeated in English, "Absolutely nothing is wrong with you, my son.
Let me tell you a story:

Samuel was a prophet in Israel. He was the same prophet who anointed the first king Israel had, King Saul. The people liked Saul because he was very tall and handsome. However, God did not like him in the end, although he was still tall and handsome. His heart was not right. Well, God sent Samuel to go and appoint another man to replace Saul as king. This tall and handsome man whom everyone loved was rejected by God. My son it is best to have everybody hate you and for God to love you, than for everyone to love you and for God to hate you.

God sent Samuel to the house of a man named Jesse from the land of Judah in Israel. Jesse had eight sons. Samuel was to anoint one, but he did not know which one. He went to the first who was tall and handsome and the eldest but God said, "No, not him!" Samuel passed from one to the other but God said, "I have not chosen any of these."
Everyone loves them. They talk very nicely and eloquently. Their noses are perfect. They are important. People look up to them, but God said, "No, I have not chosen any of these!"
Samuel asked Jesse if he had any other sons and he said, "Yes. I have one other son. His name is David. He is out in the field with the sheep."
David was out there alone and almost forgotten, doing a job no one else wanted to do. He was left out of everything important. He must have felt bullied and marginalized. He was the youngest, why was he doing all the hard work? But while he was out there, he was learning and believing everything God said about him. He became so strong in God. He believed in himself so much, in who he was in God's eyes. He wrote many things about the God he came to discover. God also got the opportunity to test him out in the field.

Samuel said to Jesse. "Go and call him, quickly!"
It was at that time that God said to Samuel, "I do not see as people see. People look on the outside to

make a judgment, I inspect the heart."
"What do you think God is saying about you?" Anansi asked John.
"He does not look at my big nose, Sir," John answered, encouraged, "He sees my heart."
"In the eyes of God, your nose is not big," Anansi said, emphasizing his point with a gesture, "It is perfect. Never let what people say about you determine how you feel about yourself!"
Anansi was silent and John was silent too.

"Do you remember the story of Jesus, where He was born?" Anansi asked.
"In a manger," John replied. "Who do you believe wants to be born in a manger with smelly animals? The animals do not use toilets. Jesus had no crib for a bed. He had to settle for hay underneath the warm cloth that they wrapped Him in. How do you think God allowed His only begotten Son to be born in such a deplorable place!

The wise men did not do anything else than to go to the king's palace first to look for this baby prince. They did not understand that he was born King. Even though they were following a star, they thought just as everyone else would expect, that a king would be born in a palace. People always get it wrong. They follow their heart and their sinful thoughts. They call things what make them comfortable because they get blinded by their own wisdom and by pride. They follow their own counsel instead of the star that was leading them all along. They cause trouble to even the best of us as they caused trouble to Jesus. Mary and Joseph were in a crisis and had to run because of people's opinion, but God shielded them.
You see John, it did not really matter where Jesus was born. It did not matter what conveniences He had at birth, and it did not matter how He looked or how much He cried and acted like a baby. What really mattered was that He was born. What mattered also is who He was and what He came to do.
The fact that He ran did not change the truth that He

was King. He was born that you.
You may find yourself on the back foot and running
but it does not change the truth about you, John.
It does not matter where you live and what you
look like John, what really matters is who you are
and the plans God has for you. You are a son of
God. God loves you very much. God has a great
big plan for your life.   Look at me
today. Who could have thought Anansi would be
like this? It did not happen over night. I was born
like this. I just never embraced it until very late. God
can make the greatest thing of you if you will allow Him. What really matters is what you carry. You
carry Jesus inside you. He is the King to whom everyone bows. He makes you extremely special and
valuable.
Only small minds get distracted by the outside. You
are very big inside and that matters."
John laughed and his mother silently applauded.
        "Now let me tell you how to handle the bul-
lies," Anansi continued.
"I am going to give you David's formula. Do you
remember the story of David and Goliath?
Goliath was the bully; a big bad one. He came out
and said bad things about Israel, then roared at
Israel and everyone ran away. This is what bullies
do, they say mean things to make you feel bad
and roar to scare you.
This makes them feel very good and important.
Goliath felt great about himself. He made himself
the most important presence on the battlefield and
anywhere around. If Goliath felt as powerful as his
roar, he would have gone up and fought Israel in
the first place. He would not have waited to win
a war with their minds. He was happy just to see
them run away.
When David came out against him he roared. He
expected David to run like everyone else. What did
David do? David did not run away, instead he ran
towards the giant.
The first thing for you to know when you are deal-

ing with bullies: Never run away from them or show that you are afraid of them. They will keep coming and picking you out if you keep running."
John laughed and his mother silently applauded.

"The second thing you should know is: you must know who you are within you: that you are strong, that God is on your side, that you are very beautiful inside, that you can be the best that you can be, that you can be greater than any of them and even greater than Anansi. You must know that God loves you just the way you are, that God loves you because of who you are and so you should love yourself. Yes, John...you must know this!

David said to this oversized bully, named...do you remember his name? Goliath right!
David said 'Who is this uncircumcised Philistine man to dare defy the army of the living God?'
David ignored his name. In fact he simply asked, who is he?
It does not matter your name, or your frame, or your position in life if you ignore the wisdom of God. If you stand against what God is standing for you are crushed. When you know the truth you stand up like David and say, 'Who are these uncircumcised ears to defy the creation of the living God? Who are these uncircumcised hearts to defy the image of the living God?'"
John gasped as the truth registered.
Anansi continued, "David knew he represented God and that with God he was powerful. It does not matter if he looked like just a boy in the giant's eyes, he was as tall as a mountain in God's eyes. He knew that if he could see himself in God's eyes, he could defeat any giant.
If God made you in His image, then anyone who says anything about your look is really criticizing the image of God."

Anansi looked into John's eyes and asked, "Does anyone have the right to criticize the work of God?"
A tear of gratitude fell from John's face as he re-

sponded, "No Sir!"

Anansi continued, "God is big enough to defend Himself. This was the secret David knew. This means you do not need to be afraid or to carry the hurts yourself. Give it to Jesus. It is His anyway."

John laughed and his once more his mother silently applauded. She did not want to interfere with this session or to distract the attention to herself. She was enjoying every moment of it though.

"The next thing you should know John, talk back to them.

David said to the giant who was shouting at him, 'You come to me with sword and shield but I come in the name of the God of Israel. It is His army you are defying.

God will deliver you into my hand today and I am going to feed you to the ravenous birds and wild beasts. Everyone on earth will know there is a God in Israel when I am through with you.'"

"You see John, bullies hate confrontation. They feed on fear. When you present the word of God as your sword and Jesus as your shield, He will defend you."

John laughed and his mother silently applauded.

Anansi looked directly at John. John was silent, pensive, taking in everything Anansi was saying to him. "You are not in the business of war, so you are not to speak bad things in anger to anyone. You must talk back to them, but not to embarrass them. An embarrassed bully will do foolish things to prove himself and regret it later.

Jesus says that the way to overcome evil is with good.

The next time someone tells you that you have a big nose, smile with that person and say, 'Yes, I admire your nose also. I see, you are made in the image of God, just as I am!'"

John laughed and his mother again silently applauded.

The song LOVE WILL PICK YOU OUT began to play softly.

John sat there quietly as Anansi offered him some fruits and nuts. The session was finished.

"Thank you, Mrs. Grace, for bringing John," Anansi said.

As John and his mother were about to go through the door to leave, Anansi called John back inside.

"See those three packages over there?" he said to John. "Choose one. Anyone you select is yours!"

The first package was very big. The wrapping was pretty and very elegant. It was very enticing to John. John's eyes fell on that package. He looked at the package beside it. It was not as big, but it also had a very nice wrapping. John's eyes kept going back to the first package. It kept pulling him as if it was a magnet. He looked at the third package and quickly glanced away. It was wrapped in newspaper and "What was that?" It appeared as if a piece of garbage was sticking out from it. John said to himself, "I must be stupid!"

The attraction of the first package became irresistible in comparison to the other two packages on offer. John looked at the first package again as the eyes of Anansi fell on him. He did not want to appear greedy to this spiritual icon.

"Take the one you want," Anansi urged, in the softest, kindest tone. "If you do not, someone else will take it anyway."

That was all the encouragement John needed. He reached out for the biggest package and felt his pulse race as it came home to its owners hands. He could hardly wait to see what nice present Anansi was giving him to take home. From the stories he heard of Anansi since he got saved, he understood that he was very generous and only gave excellent gifts.

"Why don't you open it?" Anansi urged. John could not wait to unwrap his present. He simply took the pretty package and ripped it apart.

"This is the best day of my life," he thought. "I cannot wait to sprinkle the topping on what is already the most memorable day."

John tore into the package in his excitement.
He saw a box inside. It was an ordinary box. John
placed his hand in it and "–Oops, mucky!"
John pulled his hand out and the smell was stifling.
He looked at his hand, and said with his nose wrin-
kled, the expression on his face amusingly memorable, "Rotten…rotten …rotten garbage." A piece of
slimy potato skin stuck to his fingers and a tear fell
from his eyes. John felt so bad.
"He taught me all those positive things and now…
look what he has done to me. I even thought
he liked me!" John said in his thoughts. His face
dropped with disappointment and he tried hard to
hold back the tears. He was losing the fight.
"Please, open that other one for me," Anansi said,
pointing to the third package. Anansi grimaced, hat-
ing the hurt he had caused this young man.
He knew, though, it would be only momentary. The
one he pointed to was the one with the newspaper
and the garbage sticking out.
If John was hurt before, the very suggestion of
this made him feel much worse. "Why is Anansi being so mean to me? I never expected this of him. All
the stories… all the lovely stories were lies, all lies!"
It was then that his mother intervened for the first
time. She was sitting there quietly all along, but
now, she encouraged him to do as Anansi said.
"Son, you trusted Anansi before; trust him now!"
John did not want to dishonor Anansi even
though he felt terrible.
He reached out and took the package. His mother
sighed in relief.
He opened it carefully. Trying to avoid the mess he
was sure was inside.
His eyes lit up the moment he saw the contents.
The garbage was just on the surface. Inside was a
beautiful glass box and in it was…
John caught his breath, then screamed, "Five hun-
dred US dollars!"
Inside the package was a wad of bills labeled Five

hundred dollars. He could see the currency.

"Count it!" Anansi urged.

John took the money and counted it excitedly.

His voice trembled as he whispered, "Five hundred US dollars."

He then said under his breath, "I missed out so badly."

He looked up at Anansi.

Anansi smiled and said, "You see, it is not about the package, it is what is inside!"

Anansi waited until John had regained his composure.

"What did you do with the fancy wrapping of the first package?" Anansi asked. Then answering the question himself, "You tore it up. You ripped it apart completely to get at what was inside it, right?

You gave it absolutely no regard after it guided your choice for you were settled on what was inside."

John nodded fearfully and respectfully.

"You see!" Anansi said, "It is not about how you look on the outside, it is who you are on the inside that really matters. It does not matter what your packaging is, color black, white, nose big, small, speech eloquent or slurred, scars or no scars, it is all about the Jesus in you, it is all about your heart. It is not about your nose, in the end, only what is inside matters."

John stood amazed and transfixed at the wisdom and depth of Anansi.

Anansi continued, "People always get it wrong. They go for the packaging. They mess up. That is why they overlook so much treasure. Real treasures, like the treasure in you my son.

You may keep the five hundred dollars."

"Thank you, thank you, sir!" John said excitedly. His mother was beaming.

John laughed to himself saying, "This is the most money I have ever had at any one time in my life but the lesson is so much more valuable. Anansi has given me back my life. I would have had the greatest treasure if I never got any money.

Anansi's lessons are life-saving."

As John and his mother stepped through the door to leave Anansi said to John's mother. "I will be holding a public forum on bullying soon at the town hall. All the schools in this village will be present. Ensure you come and that you bring John." John's mother nodded, perhaps a little too much, a little too hard, a little too long.

John and his mother left Anansi's house to go home. They were satisfied and fully motivated. They said nothing on their way home but their hearts were filled with joy.

John kept repeating the advice Anansi gave him as they journeyed:

1. Never run away from them or show that you are afraid of them.
2. You must know who you are within yourself, that you are strong, that God is on your side, that you are very beautiful inside, that you can be the best you can be. That you can be greater than any of them and greater than Anansi; that God loves you just the way you are, that God loves you because of who you are, and you must love yourself. Yes...you must know!
3. Talk back to them, positively.

John laughed when he thought on how he was enticed by that fancy wrapping of the big package and how quickly he tore up the wrapping paper to get at what was inside.

Just a package, he said to himself, touching his nose. He then placed his hand on his heart and was silent.

1. THE FACTS ABOUT YOU ARE NOT NECESSARILY THE TRUTH ABOUT YOU. THE TRUTH ABOUT YOU IS WHAT YOUR MAKER SAYS ABOUT YOU.
2. TRUTH OVERRIDES, OVER-WRITES AND OBLITERATES FACTS; CHOOSE TO BELIEVE THE TRUTH.
3. WHAT GOD SAYS ABOUT YOU IS THE ONLY FACT ABOUT YOU THAT IS TRUE.
4. YOU ARE INDEED FEARFULLY AND WONDERFULLY MADE IN THE IMAGE OF GOD, WORTHY OF THE DEATH OF HIS SON; YOU WERE CREATED DIFFERENT TO BE A DIFFERENCE AND WITH GOD YOU HAVE NO LIMITS; THAT IS YOUR TRUTH, AND NO FLAW, OR CIRCUMSTANCE OF YOUR LIFE CAN OVERRIDE THIS.

35

BOOK TWO

BULLYING AT SCHOOL

Victimization

CHAPTERS IN BOOK 2

THE PLOT OF EVIL

John arrived at school early. He was feeling very confident. It had been three days since he had been to Anansi and things had been so different. He was no longer conscious of his nose. In fact, he began to believe that his nose made him unique and special, and he loved himself that way. The children had noticed the change and were not teasing him anymore. John's response to them and the fact that he refused to be upset or disturbed had drawn every fight out of them. His positive attitude had made them begin to like him.

They knew he had been to Anansi and that made him a hero. It even appeared that some would not mind a big nose themselves to grab some of the spotlight he was having.

As John stepped into his classroom, he saw Jeff coming. Jeff was one of the bullies who had targeted him. Jeff had lost his confidence, but it seemed he was under great pressure from his gang of bullies to continue pestering John.

John was ready for him.

Jeff approached John before his classmates and began chanting at the top of his voice, "Big nose, Mamma big nose."

John felt sorry for him. He was now realizing that a person who seeks value from diminishing another person is the one to be pitied. Anansi had told him, "To belittle means to be little."

He felt compassion for this oversized boy with the birth mark on his cheek.

John prayed in his heart, "Lord, help me to get Your truth across to Jeff today."

Jeff appeared to have grown a little more confident by the pause. John did not cry or run away as he would before, but he had taken a moment to respond. "This is a sign of fear," Jeff thought.

Jeff said, a little louder, "Big nose, big nose, mamma big nose!"
He was very sure he had gained the upper hand this time.
John turned, looked into Jeff's eyes and said with such authority. This made Jeff catch his breath.
"I do not believe God made a mistake with you, Jeff!"
"What is this about me?" Jeff thought surprised.
"I don't believe God ever makes a mistake, do you?" John continued.

Jeff responded to the question without thinking. It was the authority and kindness with which John spoke that seemed to compel him. "Ah yes, well, aw no!" Jeff stumbled.
"That is why God likes you just the way you are, and I do too," John said.
There was silence for a few seconds, but it seemed like minutes.
"You like me?" Jeff thought. "And God? What is there to like. I am a bully. I hate...O no! How can you...?"
The moment was very awkward for Jeff. He was now confronting the real problem. He never felt anyone could like him just the way he was. He felt he needed to exert his dominance to gain acceptance. It became obvious Jeff was stumped.
He was looking sheepish. His menacing appearance completely faded, and it was as if a flicker of a smile was fighting his facade to light his face for a difference.
John seized the occasion and said in a commanding, yet, kind and measured tone, "And that is why I like my nose just the way it is."
All the students in the class cheered.

Jeff stepped out of the classroom and went into the restroom. He touched his face. He looked around to see if anyone was watching. He saw no one. He was alone.
Jeff looked into the mirror and touched the big ke-

loid growth on his cheek.

"This growth runs in my family," Jeff said to himself. "I have been so ashamed of it in the past. That is why I joined the gang. That is why I turned the laugh on others. Nobody dares to even laugh at me now.

But why have I been so ashamed of myself? John is right, God never makes a mistake."

At that moment, the door of the bathroom swung open and a group of three boys entered.

Jeff removed his hand from his face quickly. He looked up and smiled with the boys and stepped out. He hoped they had not noticed his private party. But then, how could they?

That afternoon, Jeff was detained in the class by his teacher to complete his class work. When he was released, he hurried over to the playfield to join his cronies for a game of football. This field was where the gang of bullies met in the evenings after school.

The game was already in session when Jeff arrived. His friends were happy to see him.

"Hi Donald," Jeff said, waving to the leader of the bullies who was on the field playing.

"Come join us on the field, Jeff," Donald said smiling.

Jeff quickly changed his clothes and entered the game. He played on the team with Donald and his other friends.

As they played, a small diminutive boy named Pete received the ball from his teammate. Donald rushed over to tackle and with a deft move, Pete shifted him and was past him with the ball. Donald came back at him running and he checked, pushed the ball through Donald's legs and was gone. Donald came back at him roughly with a wild kick and he skillfully avoided Donald. Donald was on his face and everyone was laughing.

This was the only time anyone could make a fool of Donald. He was the biggest and meanest of all the bullies. Pete then aimed for the goal and shot the

ball with his feet. It was a spectacular goal. Everyone was cheering for Pete and his team. They absolutely loved it. Donald would have none of it. He
got up and ran at Pete and pushed him harshly to
the floor.

It was so hard that Pete was bruised and
limping. Pete was very angry.
He appeared as if he would brave the meanness
and size of Donald and retaliate. Donald's gang of
bullies, a group of five boys including Jeff came up
and surrounded Pete menacingly and laughed.
"Pete is angry," Donald teased. "Pete is going to
fight."
Donald pushed Pete again; this time just a light
shove to make a point and to get him to retaliate.
Pete recognized the futility of fighting. He walked
away with tears in his eyes. He was feeling angry
and frustrated.

Donald and his gang of bullies went from the
playfield congratulating each other. They sat down
on a bench under a huge tree.
Richard, who was also known for his ruthlessness
leaned over to Jeff and said, "It seems you have become soft. You are not teasing John as before."
Donald chipped in at that moment. "That is true,
Jeff," he said. "What is happening little bro.? You
used to make that boy cry."
"I would swear he was about to stop coming to
school because of you," Richard continued. "That
would have been so cool."
Andy, who was feared for his quiet brutality added
his voice to the conversation. He said slowly, licking
his lips, "And you knew how to get the pack going.
You would time it to perfection.
The entire school loved that Mamma Boy song you
made.
How is it again?"
    He's a boy
    Not a toy
    He is just a mamma boy

What's his name, you suppose
Call him Mamma Big nose
See that size
Jesus Christ
The nose knows it cannot lie
What's he like
Mamma knows
Call him Mamma Big nose

All the boys in the gang began laughing uncontrollably.

Kem spoke up through his laughter, "I remember the first time he heard it, he ran from school so hard. He did not turn up again for two days."

"Yes indeed," Andy responded, "Those were your glory days.

What is happening, Jeff? It seems you have lost your touch. John is even... did I just say John? Seems I am giving him too much respect also. Big Nose is even talking back to you and looking in your face as if he is not afraid anymore."

"As if he feels he is someone important," Kem added.

Jeff sat there and was listening quietly. He liked the attention. He liked to see them laugh at his ruthless jokes on others. Something was not the same this time around though. He was not enjoying the attention. He felt ashamed and disgusted by his mean joke and to hear them repeat it was more painful to him than it was uplifting.

Jeff hung his head slightly as he responded. "I don't know man. When John speaks, he does not speak about himself or his nose, he speaks about me. He tells me I am made in the image of God, and I am a wonderful person."

Jeff spoke this in undertones, his eyes looking down as if ashamed.

"Plus you all know it is no fun to mock someone who is not afraid of being mocked. It takes away all the fun and logics of bullying."

Jeff looked up, speaking more confidently and resolutely as he continued, "If I am made in the image of God, then John is also. I cannot accept it for myself without seeing him also. Is God wicked to give him a big nose? God is always good. It makes it difficult for me to call him Big Nose anymore."

Everyone was silent all this time Jeff spoke. The silence continued for a short while after. The bullies digested what he had spoken.

It was Donald who broke the silence, "Do you want us to gang him?"

Kem joined the conversation then, "O yes," he said. "Let us beat the confidence out of him. He will become a wimp once more."

"Great idea Kem," Richard spoke up laughing. "Perhaps he will go harm himself. Rid us of that jerk forever."

Jeff added a word of caution, "Gotta be careful man. People are starting to like him. They will hate us if we touch him. They may even turn on us."

"And I have heard that he has been speaking to Anansi," Kem said.

At the name Anansi, they were all silent.

"Anansi," everyone repeated, almost speaking together in reverence.

Even these bullies harbored dreams of meeting with Anansi someday. Their aggression gave them status built on fear, but they knew meeting with Anansi is the greatest prestige any student could boast of.

"If this is true, if he has met Anansi, he is in 'A' class now," Andy said

"If only I could meet Anansi!" Kem and Richard said, airing their thoughts almost concurrently.

"John seems to believe that his relationship with God is more important than his relationship with Anansi." Jeff said. "He thinks that because God made him as he is, he should be very proud of it, big nose and everything else. I have even heard that he said that God is able to defend him against those who offend him without a cause."

Andy, somewhat disturbed by the conversation,

said, "Let us forget about John. He is trouble. Let us focus on the others."

This gang was a bunch of troublemakers who took pride in causing pain and trouble. They fed on the weakness of children who could not defend themselves. The others Andy was referring to was a number of unpopular children they were preying on.

Kem immediately accepted Andy's offer to change the topic.

"I don't know how Peter's mother does it, but his lunch certainly tastes good," he said, touching his belly for emphasis.

Donald began licking his lips then. "It is a whopper!" he said, "I am getting hungry."

"Sometimes I get sorry for Peter," he added. "He has not had any of his own lunch for at least three weeks now."

"Sorry?" Kem asked sarcastically.

"Sorry," Donald said, "sorry he does not have money we could take away too."

All the bullies laughed

"You guys are very terrible," Andy said still laughing, "Peter is really getting a beating. He knows if he complains, he will get the real beating. He will run into us."

"O yes!" Kem said, "We will have him for lunch." These bullies could not have known Peter's mother was very poor. Peter sometimes had no dinner. Lunch was a major sacrifice.

They could not have known, but if they did, they would not care.

Richard spoke up, changing the subject, "You should see the look on Andrew's face when I pushed him down in front the girls. He was so embarrassed." Richard made a face mimicking the shame and embarrassment and howled as the others laughed.

It was Jeff who countered. "Don't you think that is a dangerous game? Andrew has very serious asthma. I heard he had to be rushed to the hospital the last time you attacked him."

"The greater the drama, the sweeter the feeling," Andy said.

"And the more news we make," Kem added. "He is a geek anyway. Everyone hates him and is also jealous of him."

Richard agreed, "Even those who take his side publicly are secretly cheering us on. They want us to whip the geek out of him."

"On a serious note," Jeff said, "What if Andrew has a serious asthma attack because of this?"

"You worry too much," Richard said. "If that ever happens, we will deal with it when it comes."

Alex the womanizer who was silent all along spoke up, "Sonia still refuses to go out with me."

"Don't worry about that, Alex," Donald said. "I have a bunch of popular girls on her case. Sharon, Lavern, Susan aah!"

Everyone nodded in approval and smiles broke out on their faces.

"Their job is to pester Sonia about her virginity until she gives in," Donald continued. "You will have her run to you crying for affection soon Alex!"

"What am I to do?" Alex said.

"Trust is the word," Donald said. "Let her feel she can trust you."

"Anything is the verb," Donald added. "When the time comes do anything you desire."

"Awesome!" Alex exclaimed. "I will be the perfect friend and first person at hand when she caves in. Popularity always wins."

"I am off," Donald said, getting up from his seat. "I have a project to turn in tomorrow."

Donald moved from person to person touching hands with every member of the group. "Let us show them who rules this school.

The group nodded, and they all got up and dispersed.

1. WE MUST NEVER BE FOOLED, GOD IS NOT MOCKED;
   WE FOOL OURSELVES, AND MOCK OUR FUTURE IF WE
   IGNORE THIS.
2. IT MAY SEEM RIGHT AT THE TIME BUT IF IT CON-
   TRADICTS THE WORD IT IS WRONG; IT MAY SEEM
   LIKE LIFE, BUT IF IT IS CONTRARY TO THE WORD
   IT IS DEATH.
3. CONSIDER YOUR ACTIONS CAREFULLY; YOUR PRESENT
   ACTIONS ARE A PRESENTATION OF YOUR FUTURE.

MILTON MAYE

PETER SPEAKS UP

The morning sun had risen in the sky as Peter and his mother stood in the front yard of their small house. Peter had not discussed his ordeal at school over the past weeks with his mother. How could he let her know that the bullies were taking away his lunch after all the sacrifices she was making? Somehow, it was unfair to her. Peter was tortured by the bullies and tortured by his conscience for withholding information from his mother.

Today, it would be very different. That night he had heard a program that encouraged him to stand up to the bullies. To share his experience with someone he trusted. Today he would take a step, even a very small one.

As Mrs. Grace handed Peter his lunch kit, Peter said to his mother, "I am not taking lunch to school today, mother."

Concern immediately flushed Mrs. Grace's face. This was not like Peter. Lunch was his best meal.

"Why Peter?" Mrs. Grace asked.

Peter paused for a while. It appeared he had lost his confidence. He decided to change the subject.

"Mother, did you see my test results, I got perfect A's!"

Mrs. Grace was even more concerned now. She rebuked him sternly with anxiety in her voice, "Peter!" There was silence.

"Peter," Mother said again, "I am so proud of you, but do not change the subject, son.

"I am very proud of your performance at school, but why have you decided not to take lunch?"

Peter paused. He said to himself, "I hate to tell Mother this. Mother is such a beautiful person. I don't want her to worry.

Daddy would know what to do but he is away. He is always away working, but never having enough to provide for us."

Peter knew he had to answer. He blurted it out, not sure how his mother would respond, "The boys are taking away my lunch."

His mother's response was that of a typical mother. "What!" Mrs. Grace exclaimed.

After seeing the look of dismay on Peter's face, she softened her tone.

"What did you say my son?" she asked in a soft understanding voice.

"The boys are taking away my lunch," Peter repeated. "Kem and the others force me to give them my lunch every day."

Mrs. Grace responded, her voice a measure of controlled anxiety. "How long has this been happening?"

"For some time now," Peter answered. "But for the past three weeks, I have not had lunch one day." Peter could not control himself anymore. He began sobbing. This broke his mother's heart. Mrs. Grace hugged him close to her.

While he cried, Mrs. Grace, whose face was hidden above Peter's head, was weeping inside. Her face was contorted, but she held back the tears. She felt anger, frustration and concern, all mixed in the tears welling up in her eyes. She would not allow Peter to see how she was feeling but in that moment she was all feelings. She could not put her thoughts together.

Mrs. Grace held onto Peter, giving him her support but also to give herself time to recover. Finally, she gained enough control to respond. Her voice was shaking as she said, "Did you tell it to teacher?"

"No mother," Peter responded.

"Why didn't you tell me before?" his mother agonized.

"They threatened me that if I told it to anyone they would beat me severely," Peter answered sobbing.

"What!" Mother exclaimed very concerned, now. She quickly regained her composure.

"What my son!" she said softly.

"They mean it," Peter said to his mother. "It is a group of them and they beat up students all the time."

"Let me pray about it!" Mrs. Grace said.

Peter had come to love his mother for this. When she did not have an answer for any situation, she would pray and somehow it would work out good.

Mother kissed Peter and said, "Go to school now son. I will keep your lunch for you. I will tell you what I will do when you return."

Mother watched until Peter was out of sight, then she collapsed into a chair and began to weep.

> My tears flow freely
> Day and night
> They have been my meat
> While they say unto me
> Where is the God you seek?
> When I think on these things
> I pour out my soul inside
> I'm panting, I'm thirsty
> I'm thirsty and dry
>
> Thirsty and dry
> Thirsty and dry
> And panting am I
> As a hart for the brooks
> As a hart pants for water
> Lord hear my cry
> Deep calls to deep
> Depths that can't be denied
> I'm hungry, I'm panting
> I'm thirsty and dry

Peter's mother lay down on the chair feeling weak for about two hours. She could not speak or pray. She was powerless to get up. What Peter said had left her totally drained.

After some time, Mrs. Grace, mustered the strength to rise up and began to pray.

Mrs. Grace said to God exhaustedly, "Lord You know we can barely make ends meet. I try to give Peter at least one good meal every day and that is lunch. I want him to remain interested in school. Now this!" She continued through her tears, "I even have to borrow many times to be able to afford lunch. Sometimes, we do without dinner. How could this be happening? How could this be happening? How could this be happening?" The voice of Mrs. Grace trailed off into silence.

Time passed as Mrs. Grace remained in her position on the chair agonizing and groaning.

It was about midday when she shifted her position. She was feeling stronger and more hopeful by the time she opened her Bible. She turned to the scripture in Philippians 4:6 and began repeating softly:

> "Do not be anxious for anything
> In everything by prayer and giving of thanks
> Tell God what you want Him to do.
> Do not be anxious for anything
> In everything by prayer and giving of thanks
> Tell God what you want Him to do."

Mrs. Grace prayed, "Lord, I want You to let the bullies at school respect Peter and leave his lunch alone. I want You also to change the heart of the bullies. Make them honest, respectful, respectable, secure and give them a sense of purpose and life."

It was lunch time at school. Just as they had done the previous weeks, the bullies came and surrounded Peter as soon as the teacher had left the classroom. The other children saw what was happening, but they appeared to pay no attention. They did not want to be picked on themselves so they stayed out of it.

Kem took Peter's bag from beside him as Peter sat

petrified. He looked but did not see his lunch kit.
"There is no lunch kit here," Kem said.
"Let me see," Donald demanded. When he saw Peter did not have his lunch, he scattered all the contents of the bag on the ground. Andy pushed Peter who fell to the ground in his chair. They all walked away.
Peter picked himself up, putting his head on the desk and he began to cry.
Mrs. Grace felt joy enter her heart. The sure solution came to her in that moment.
She whispered to herself, "Ah yes! Ah yes! Anansi. Thank You Jesus!"
The solution became so real to her in that moment that she screamed, "Anansi yes, Anansi!"
Mrs. Grace quickly went to the bathroom, got dressed and hurriedly left the house. She wanted to return before Peter arrived home that evening.

---

1. YOUR GOD WILL TURN YOUR MOURNING TO DANCING AND YOUR SORROWS TO LAUGHTER. HIS PROMISE TO YOU IS: WHEN YOU WALK THROUGH THE WATERS I WILL BE WITH YOU, AND THROUGH THE FIRE I WILL BE WITH YOU.

2. GOD CAN TURN YOUR TEST INTO A TESTIMONY, A TESTAMENT OF HIS GOODNESS; GOD WILL TURN YOUR MESS INTO A MESSAGE.

3. JESUS IS CONSTANTLY SAYING, "CAST YOUR CARES ON ME, I DO CARE FOR YOU."

ANANSI'S DISCIPLINE

Anansi was in his regular time of study and devotion. He was there for almost two hours, and he was feeling uplifted. He lifted his hands and danced in worship to his favorite worship song, HOLY SPIRIT LEAD THE WAY. It was the song they sung at church when he got saved. Anansi opened his Bible and began to study. He was reading for about thirty minutes before he closed the Bible.

Anansi began to dance to the song NOT ENOUGH MOMENTS

NOT ENOUGH MOMENTS IN THE NIGHT
NOT ENOUGH MOMENTS IN THE DAY
NOT ENOUGH TIME TO LOVE YOU RIGHT
IN OUR SECRET GET AWAY
NOT ENOUGH TIME TO REST AT WILL
NOT ENOUGH TIME TO BE ALONE
LORD LET THE MOON BE STILL
SO I CAN LOVE YOU MORE AND MORE
NOT ENOUGH MOMENTS IN THE NIGHT
NOT ENOUGH MOMENTS IN THE DAY
TOO SOON THE SUN WILL RISE
TOO SOON I'M CALLED AWAY
I AM CALLED AWAY

The song stopped and Anansi began a rhythmic recital as he stood up. He was thinking about what people had said about him. That he was born wise. Anansi said:

"So they think Anansi was born wise more than anyone else
Oh no! I develop my craft
So they think I am gifted above the rest
O no! I work for what I have, O yes
I study to show myself approved

I read the word, and I read books
When I don't know I simply ask
My companion Deep is equal to the task."

What Anansi really meant was that he prayed for at least one hour every day. On most days, Anansi prayed and studied the Bible for at least three hours.
He reads at least five chapters of the Bible everyday but many times he reads between ten and twenty chapters.
Anansi's secret is that he believes the word of God as it is stated in Psalms 1. He really took the word of God literally. The Bible says if you meditate in the Word day and night, you will be blessed and everything you do will prosper.
He also considered himself an understudy of every successful man of God in the Bible: Abraham, Moses, David, Daniel, Peter and the others. He concluded that they all loved the presence of God and did whatever it took to pursue it and to stay in it.
Anansi also consulted and researched every topic he was to address. He had a mechanical friend by the name of Deep.
Deep was an interactive computer with mechanical Anansi legs and a face that looked like a scroll.
Deep allowed Anansi to research any topic at the touch of a button or by a voice command or instruction.
Anansi's computer had its own personality also. It had a very funny laugh "Haw, haw, haw; hee, he, he, he; hee, he, he, he" and had an exciting way of responding to him.
He turned to Deep and said, "My friend, Deep, dig deep and give a wise answer to me.
Deep tell me, what drives a bully?"
Deep returned the response to Anansi in his own fun parabolic manner:
"Drives...? Well yes, drives.
A bully is a car without an engine
They are driven by a concept and not by reality

They have potential but they have little heart
They are regressive and not progressive
A bully is like a lovely mango full of worms
They present themselves for beauty and
importance, but they cannot be digested
Give a bully a heart and a bully's life will start."

Deep laughs: "Haw, haw, haw; hee, he, he, he; hee, he, he, he."
He continued, "It is like giving a car an engine.
Give a bully compassion and it will change
his life forever.
The car will now take the road and be
a blessing to its driver."
Deep laughs again, "Haw, haw, haw; hee,
he, he he hee, he, he he
Your answer is found in the greatest
commandment ever:
Love the Lord with all your heart
And love your neighbor as yourself
Everyone who bullies lacks compassion and
love."
Deep was silent and inanimate once again.
Anansi was silent for a minute:
Anansi prayed in response to Deep. "Lord how can I apply this knowledge to help bullies?"
He then began to pray one of his favorite scriptures from Psalms 91, "He who dwells in the secret place of the Most High shall certainly abide under His shadow.
I want to live under Your shadow Lord; overshadow me. I crave proximity. Lord overshadow me."
Anansi left his study dancing to the song that had become his mission statement, FIFTY DOLLAR NOTE.

1. GOD'S INSTRUCTIONS TO JOSHUA: DO NOT LET THE WORD OF GOD DE-PART FROM YOUR MOUTH, MEDITATE IN IT DAY AND NIGHT AND YOU WILL HAVE GOOD SUCCESS – JOSHUA 1

2. DAVID'S INSTRUCTION TO US FROM HIS OWN PERSONAL EXPERIENCE: IF YOU MEDITATE IN THE WORD OF GOD DAY AND NIGHT EVERYTHING YOU DO WILL PROSPER (WHATEVER) – PSALMS 1

ANDREW HOSPITALIZED

The group of bullies, denied lunch, stormed from Peter's classroom. They were angry. They were angry with Peter. They were angry because of Peter. They were angry because they were one lunch less today.

Kem turned to the others and said, "Boy, I am hungry. Where am I going to get lunch now? Peter was easy picking. I wonder what happened?"

Richard responded, shaking his fist, "I am mad!" Richard then addressed the group, "Let us take it out on someone else. Someone must pay, and I know the perfect person."

Kem looked at Richard knowingly, "Andrew?" he quipped.

Richard nodded to the affirmative.

"I wonder if he has money," Kem said.

"You will find out real soon," Richard promised.

Jeff who had suddenly become the conscience of the group said, "No stealing man, that is serious."

Richard responded to him, "Who is brave enough to tell on us?"

Richard began to smile deceptively, "Even then I will ensure he gives it to us voluntarily. We will not be stealing."

"Oh yes!" Donald said with a big smile. "He will hand it over by himself, we will not be stealing."

The group of bullies went out searching for Andrew. At that moment John walked by.

Jeff turned to John and started, "Big No..." He caught himself as John flashed him the biggest smile.

John then said to him, ignoring the presence of all the other bullies, "Have a great day Jeff."

Jeff looked away and the other boys chuckled.

Donald said to Jeff as John disappeared, "He has you for good Jeff."

Richard commented also, "I must admit, I am enjoying his new confidence."

It was then that they saw Andrew up the road. Richard said quietly, "Hey guys, there is Andrew. Let us pretend we are not interested in him, as if we do not notice him."

Kem said, "Yes, he will provide my lunch today or we will have him for lunch."

Donald took command at that moment. He said, "Drop back a little Richard. I will walk on ahead so I can be behind him to cut off his escape."

Everyone dropped back as Donald proceeded past Andrew.

Kem went forward and bounced Andrew on the shoulder.

Kem spoke to him discreetly in that moment, "Give me everything in your pocket and ensure you do it with a smile."

Andrew looked in front of him and saw how bad the situation was. Richard and Andy nodded at him. Richard faked a smile.

Andrew looked behind him to his escape route and saw Donald. Donald nodded and faked a smile.

Kem looked at Andrew and said, "Do it with a smile now or else!"

Andrew managed a weak fearful smile and Richard laughed.

"Keep that smile going," Kem said. "You are with friends. Now put your hand into your pocket and give over everything!" he commanded threateningly.

Andrew put his hand in his pocket but hesitated. He then looked around as if still looking for a way to escape.

It was at this point that Richard lost patience. He would not tolerate this hesitation.

Richard slammed his fist into Andrew's chest so hard, the impact could be heard.

He immediately regretted it. Andrew fell to the

ground with a heavy thud.
His chest tightened, and he began to gag and wheeze. He looked as if he would die.
The bullies did not know what to do. They all ran away.

> My tears flow freely
> Day and night
> They have been my meat
> While they say unto me
> Where is the God you seek?
> When I think on these things
> I pour out my soul inside
> I'm panting, I'm thirsty
> I'm thirsty and dry

As Andrew writhed on the ground gasping for breath, an eyewitness who was observing in the distance ran to his assistance.
When she realized how bad the situation was she ran for help.
People came running immediately and the school nurse took charge of the situation. The sound of the ambulance grew louder in the distance. It was not long before it arrived.
Andrew was rushed to the hospital for emergency treatment. He was immediately placed on oxygen as the medics surrounded him. His condition was life threatening. He needed life support.
They quickly placed Andrew in the Intensive Care Unit of the hospital in an attempt to save his life.

---

3. *IT IS EASY TO GIVE TROUBLE, ANYONE CAN DO IT; IT TAKES COURAGE TO DO WHAT IS RIGHT.*

4. *THE TROUBLE YOU DISPLAY IS A REFLECTION OF THE WEAKNESS YOU HIDE.*

5. *YOU WILL NEVER BE ABLE TO RUN FAST ENOUGH FROM YOUR FUTURE; IT IS ALWAYS AHEAD OF YOU. ENSURE YOU CREATE THE FUTURE TODAY YOU WANT TO FIND WHEN YOU GET THERE.*

THE GRIEF OF BULLYING

None of the bullies returned to class that day. They were nowhere to be found. They realized the enormity of the situation and they were in hiding. The atmosphere was filled with concern and anxiety at school for the rest of the afternoon and no class returned to normalcy. Some of the teachers were away at the hospital. Everyone was distracted and the principal felt compelled to dismiss school a half hour early.

After school, everyone was talking about Andrew in groups. Some were speculating that he would die.

Peter did not stop to engage in the conversation. He felt very sorry for Andrew but because of what happened to him earlier at lunch time, he felt safer at home.

Peter walked home. He was so hungry that he touched his stomach and grimaced. He declined the invitation to engage the picturesque scenery of the Jamaican mountainous countryside landscape blended with the beach and the coconut trees that evening as he returned home. He would not divert to play with the sand or even to dip his bare feet in the salty water.

As Peter reached home, his mother greeted him with a big warm hug. Her face was smiling as she placed his lunch before him. It was such a different picture from that of the distraught mother he had left at home that morning.

It was a hungry Peter who sat down to lunch. He gulped his food down in appreciation. It was the tastiest meal he had ever had.

He said to his mother as he ate, "Mother, this is the best meal I have had in weeks."

Peter was not joking. Mrs. Grace had made lunch

the best meal for Peter but he was not the one to benefit.

She was somber as she acknowledged him, "I know Peter and I will ensure you have at least one best meal every day from now on."

Peter then raised the topical issue of Andrew. He said to his mother, "Mother, do you remember Andrew?"

"The top boy at school?" Mrs. Grace responded.

"Yes," Peter said. "He is in the hospital. They say his life is in danger."

"What! What happened?" Mrs. Grace said, alarmed.

"Richard and the others bullied him and triggered a severe asthma attack," Peter said.

"They say Richard will go to jail. Serves him right!"

"No Peter, we must not hate," his mother said. "Jesus teaches us to pray for those who treat us badly and who do evil things to us.

These are some serious times for Andrew and his family, for Richard and his family and for the entire school. Let us pray!"

They both bowed their heads and closed their eyes.

Mrs. Grace began to pray, "Lord, please heal Andrew. Raise him up from the hospital bed and return him to his family safely.

Richard is a bully but You love him. Help him to regret the foolish thing he has done and change him, but do not fail to deliver him from jail. You bore his punishment on the cross, so now give him Your freedom. I pray You grant him total pardon from going to jail, which he is afraid of, and total freedom from his cell of hatred and trouble making which he seems to love. Amen."

Peter responded to his mother's prayer by saying, "Amen."

He knew this was the heart of Jesus, and he loved his mother for following Jesus, especially in difficult situations.

Mother surprised Peter at that moment. She looked at him with a big smile on her face. He

could not understand her high spirit because of the gravity of his situation. But then she said, "You have an appointment with Anansi tomorrow."
Peter could not believe what he was hearing. Now, it all made sense.
He laughed, put his hand over his mouth, acted surprised, then jumped and began to dance.

Peter chanted:
> "Anansi, Anansi
> Appointment with Anansi
> Anansi, Anansi
> God bless Anansi
> God bless Anansi good, good
> God bless Anansi

He hugged his mother.
> MAMMA YOU WERE THERE WHEN I WAS
> HARDLY IN CONTROL
> YOU BORE WITH MY WEAKNESS AND
> THE TROUBLES OF MY SOUL
> NEVER ONCE DID YOU GIVE UP
> THOUGH THE EYES COULD NOT HAVE KNOWN
> WHAT YOU SAW IN ME, HATS OFF
> TO THE POWER OF LOVE
> > MAMMA - TEEN CHALLENGE JAMAICA

In the meantime, Andrew's parents were anxiously holding on in the waiting room of the hospital. They had joined a gathering of teachers who were already there.
Everyone was engaged in their own conversations. Some were praying. Andrew's Sunday School teacher and his pastor were in the waiting room also. Their presence had brought a sense of calm to everyone.

A group of Andrew's classmates was gathered outside the hospital, hoping to get some news.
"Do you believe he will live?" one asked.
Another classmate responded, "I am not sure, he is in ICU. They say his chances are slim."

The first classmate offered a prayer in that moment, "Please God, help Andrew. Geek or not he deserves life."

A third classmate entered the conversation at that point, "He was a good person, always helpful. We were just jealous of him because of his discipline. He does not deserve this."

The second classmate answered, "I know. And he always got the highest grades. The teachers praised him, and he was always the best behaved."

The first classmate to speak responded again, "They called him, Goody Goody, but is anything wrong with being good?"

The third classmate answered, "Absolutely nothing. How could we appreciate Jesus if there is some-thing wrong with being good? He was exemplary good."

The first classmate continued, "The people did not like Jesus in His day. They crucified Him."

There was silence for a moment as the three digested what they had just said.

"Lord help us! Lord help Andrew!" The second classmate exclaimed prayerfully. She appeared to be conscience-stricken for being jealous of Andrew in the past.

They looked somber and disturbed as they depart-ed to their respective homes. The conversation was sparse as each of the three walked home together in quiet reflection.

> 1. *IT IS BEST, LESS PAINFUL, AND LESS COSTLY TO LEARN FROM INSTRUCTIONS THAN TO LEARN FROM CORRECTIONS; EITHER WAY, YOU WILL BE TAUGHT TO LEARN.*
>
> 2. *IF THE RIDE IS TOO FAST, THE CRASH CAN BE DISASTROUS. BULLYING IS A COLLISION COURSE; CONSIDER THE CONSEQUENCES OF YOUR ACTIONS!*

BULLIES SCARED AND IN TROUBLE

The sound of sirens could be heard as the police arrived at Richard's home.

He was hiding in the closet trembling. He was no longer the brave bully. He had forgotten the script for the part he played at school among his gang of friends.

A female corporal headed the team of police. No one knew Richard was at home and so when his mother answered the door she said, "Richard is not home yet."

Richard's father had joined Andrew's parents at the hospital to offer support.

The police insisted on searching the house and Richard's mother permitted them. To her surprise, Richard was found shaking and frightened hiding in the closet.

His voice was trembling and almost broken as he addressed the police corporal. "I am very sorry, ma'am!"

"You should have thought about that before you assaulted Andrew," the police woman responded. "So you think that you are sorry, you certainly will be!"

> WALKING IN THE PATH OF DESTRUCTION
> REMOVE YOUR FOOT FROM EVERY EVIL WAY
> YOU WILL NOT FALL INTO CORRUPTION
> HE'S BUILDING YOU LIKE BLOCKS EVERY DAY
> KNOW THAT YOU ARE UNDER CONSTRUCTION
> AND IF YOU WILL DO WHAT HE SAYS
> GIVE YOUR EARS TO HIS INSTRUCTIONS
> LEANING ON THE LORD THERE IS CHANGE
>
> CHANGE - TEEN CHALLENGE JAMAICA

What seemed to be a wet patch appeared on Richard's trousers.

He looked at the police officer and asked, "Is...is he dead?"

The police officer responded, "Not yet Richard. Do you know how to pray?"

"God does not listen to me anymore," Richard responded.

It was then the policewoman said to him, "Then go make it right with Him. You need God's help now. It suits you to pray Richard."

Richard was taken away in handcuffs accompanied by his mother in a police car. His mother could not hold back her tears.

The car arrived at the police station after a few minutes with sirens blazing all the way.

Richard was placed in a holding area at the police station. He trembled uncontrollably as the vision of the days ahead in prison frightened him. His future was destroyed.

Kem, who was hiding in the distance watched the police take Richard away. His heart fell. He kept repeating to himself, "Mi inna trouble now. Trouble, trouble, big trouble! Laad wha mi guh duh. Mi inna trouble now?"

Kem decided to run away to escape. He was afraid of being taken to jail. He was afraid of the embarrassment. He was afraid of the prisoners. He was afraid of the dark cold lonely nights without freedom. He was running to safety. He did not know where safety was, but he would get there, so he kept running.

Kem ran himself to exhaustion. He found solace at a quiet place in the woods. It was not ideal, but he was exhausted. It was also some distance from his home. He felt they would not find him there today.

Kem began mumbling to himself repeatedly, "What have I done? I am in trouble now. They took Richard away. They will come for me for sure."

He fell asleep feeling the heat of fear for the first time. This was a time his gang could not protect him. He was dripping with sweat and the soft grass was the only comfort he had. The only shoulder present for him to rest on was the soft shoulder of the grass banking. Or to be more correct the hard ground of the path in the woods padded in grass. He was not disturbed by the pig scratching the earth in the distance. He was too distracted to see, what appeared to be a snake, hanging from a limb to his left. He was fast asleep within seconds.

Kem's parents were very concerned about him. The school's guidance counselor had come by. They had worked out an agreement with the police.

No one knew where Kem was. As the hours dragged on, they became more and more worried.

Kem woke up just after midnight. He yawned and wondered, "Where am I?"

It was then the reality came back to haunt him. A tremor passed through his body as he said, "I am in deep trouble!"

Fear returned to his face as he screamed, "O my God! I am in deep trouble, now. I am going to jail!"

He knew he could not stay there. He would need a better plan. He decided to sneak home while it was dark to get provisions and to leave the community for a while.

Kem cautiously made his way home. He kept scouting the area to ensure it was clear. He wanted to make sure the police were not waiting for him.

He could see his house in the distance. The breadfruit tree in his front yard waved at him invitingly. His spirit lifted. This was home. His spirit dropped as he whispered, "Not anymore."

He cautiously circled his home and nothing moved. There was no sign of anyone or of any police cars. Kem made his way furtively to the rear door of his house and pushed it. It was closed. He knocked quietly.

He could see the lights were on and so he peeped through a window. His mother and father were up pacing the floor.

Kem quietly knocked on the window then on the back door.

His father answered. Joy flooded his face when he saw Kem. The smile was bigger than Kem had ever experienced. He was happy to see Kem. He hugged him with a hug that told the passion he had for Kem. It was a hug Kem never experienced before. It was the relationship that was absent between them that flooded the moment. It made the situation even more bizarre. He could have never guessed his father liked him this much. This was why he was in trouble in the first place.

Kem loved it and would have liked to hold on, but he knew it would be fleeting. He would soon be in jail anyway. His father should have considered giving him this attention before. Now he would be running.

"Where were you Kem?" his father asked. "We had just called the police to report you missing."

Kem looked startled and began trembling.

His father calmed him down while his mother patted his back.

"We love you," his father said. "What is the matter, Kem? Are you in trouble again?"

He already knew the answer, but he wanted Kem to relate it.

Kem surrendered and began explaining, "I am a part of the group of bullies who harassed Richard and sent him to the hospital. I hear he may die. I saw the police take Andrew away, and I am afraid they will be coming for me next. I ran away."

"Don't worry," his mother said. "The police are not interested in you. Well... we had to agree to get counseling for you, and you will have to take the steps to change."

"We will seek to get a session with Anansi," his father said.

Kem's fear changed to relief and then to excitement and anticipation as he heard of Anansi.

"Anansi," Kem said reverentially. "Wow! That would be nice."

"Please make every effort," he said excitedly.

"Thanks, Daddy. I will make the change."

DONALD'S CALLOUSNESS

Donald knew what had happened to Andrew. He knew his friend Richard was in jail. He knew the severity of the situation but Donald was defiant.

"I am not afraid of anything or anyone," Donald said to himself as he prepared himself for school the next morning.

"So what about Richard? I will continue to do whatever I want at school. All the students will fear and respect me.

They will respect me even more when they see that this incident does not even faze me. Instead of getting better I will get, yes... better...better and more blatant at my craft."

Donald laughed. It was the sinister laughter of someone who had sold himself to evil so much that he had lost all sense of remorse.

As he headed for school, a small boy walked by. He saw Donald and passed by on the other side of the road.

Sensing fear, Donald made as if to catch him. He ran. Donald laughed.

This motivated Donald, and he felt ready for his day as the master of evil.

BULLIES ARE EVER READY FOR TROUBLE BUT NEVER READY TO FACE THE CONSEQUENCES WHEN THE TIME COMES.

BULLIES ARE EVER READY TO GIVE TROUBLE BUT NEVER READY TO FACE TROUBLE.

RICHARD'S CLOSE CALL

Richard sat at the police station in the holding area. There were other prisoners there being checked in.

Richard overheard a police officer say, "He is a juvenile but if Andrew is dead we will book him for murder."

Richard did not hear clearly what was being said, but he heard the words 'Andrew' and 'dead.'

Richard's face was full of concern as he repeated beneath his breath, "Andrew...dead!"

He could hear that strange song ROULETTE playing through the window.

TAKE THE GUN
PLACE IT TO YOUR HEAD
THEY WILL SAY THAT YOU'RE NOT CLEVER
IT'S NOT A TRICK
ONE WILL END UP DEAD
THERE IS A LIVE ROUND TO BE TRIGGERED
FOUR ARE GONE THEY ARE LUCKY
THEY SOUGHT FORGIVENESS
AND ESCAPED JUST IN TIME
TWO ARE LEFT ONE WON'T MAKE IT
IS THE BULLET YOURS OR MINE

A STAKE IS ON YOUR LIFE
YOU DON'T KNOW THE TIME YOU DIE
YOU GAMBLE WITH TOMORROW
AN ACCIDENT
ANOTHER BET, ANOTHER TRY
KNOW THE TIME IS BORROWED
NEAR MISSES MANY TIMES
GETTING O SO CLOSE
YOU REFUSE TO GIVE YOUR LIFE

YOU'RE JUST ONE OF THOSE

Standing in the cold
Playing Russian roulette
With your soul

Richard dropped to his knees and cried, "O Lord! Andrew dead. O my God! I wish I could take back that fist."

Richard had fallen on the wounded foot of a big burly detainee who was also a youth. He doubled his fist and was about to give it impulsively to Richard. His prayers were being answered in ways he could not imagine. As the detainee was about to discharge his big hand, another prisoner sitting beside him held onto it.

He looked at the angry big fellow and said, "Calm it man! We are already in big trouble! No need to make it worse."

This big guy listened as the other prisoner smiled at Richard and said in his mind, "You certainly wouldn't be able to take that one back."

Then the song came home to him:

A stake is on your life
You don't know the time you die
You gamble with tomorrow
An accident
Another bet, another try
Know the time is borrowed
Near misses many times
Getting O so close
You refuse to give your life

You're just one of those
Standing in the cold
Playing Russian roulette
With your soul

The game is very dangerous
The playing is for keeps
No man knows the hour
Whose bullet this shall be

The rich man builds his bigger barns
I'm sure you will concur
Natural or unnatural
Accidents occur

Roulette - Clive Warren

> 1. YOU GIVE TROUBLE BECAUSE YOU NEVER TRULY UNDERSTAND TROUBLE UNTIL YOU GET TROUBLE, OR RATHER UNTIL TROUBLE GETS YOU.
> 2. YOU SOW TO THE WIND YOU REAP THE WHIRLWIND. EXERCISE CONTROL NOW BECAUSE YOU CAN DO NOTHING WHEN YOUR WORLD IS SPINNING OUT OF YOUR CONTROL.

PETER VISITS ANANSI

Anansi woke up the following morning and started his daily morning routine. He danced to the tune TO BE HAPPY.

THE PRICE OF LAUGHTER WHO CAN PAY
BRING THE HEART OUT ANY DAY
WHEN THE HEART GOES OUT TO PLAY
YOU'VE GOT LAUGH TO GIVE AWAY
ITS WORTH IT
A MERRY HEART IT WILL ENRAPTURE
HAVE NO NEED TO CALL THE DOCTOR
LIKE A SPRING WITHIN
IS A JOYOUS SOUL
ITS WORTH IT

IT'S WORTH IT TO BE HAPPY
GO TELL IT TO SOMEBODY
IT'S WORTH IT TO BE HAPPY
IT'S WORTH IT
To BE HAPPY - VENECIA (SIS. PRECIOUS) STONE

He went jogging on a track in the picturesque hills. It was a time for him to unwind physically as he maintained good physical health. As he jogged, he meditated on the Word of God.

Anansi returned after about forty minutes and sat under a tree relaxing. He then went swimming for about fifteen minutes, after which, he went inside to get dressed.

He was expecting Peter and Mrs. Grace this morning and as was his custom, he had prepared for them.

Peter and Mrs. Grace woke up early in the morning. They had a time of prayer. The glow of the golden sunshine on the trees outside brought a certain sense of hope and anticipation to their day. It could not compare, however, to the glow that radiated from their hearts and the kinetic energy they felt radiating from them both at this special appointment with Anansi.

Mrs. Grace and Peter had a cup of tea before leaving home. They could not afford breakfast that morning. The fare to Anansi would take up all their resources. They had an early appointment, and they had to take two buses. The pair of mother and son was ready and on their way early.

Peter and his mother walked hand in hand all the way to the bus stop. They were fully aware of the inquisitive eyes watching them from behind the curtains. Mrs. Grace knew they must be wondering why Peter was not going to school and what they were doing all dressed up and going out.
Peter squeezed his mother's hand and said, "Thanks Mamma!"

The bus they were waiting on came after ten minutes. Peter sat down beside Mrs. Grace and hugged her in appreciation as the song Mamma played.
The bus came to a stop at the first terminus and they boarded another bus to the neighborhood of Anansi.
Peter nodded to the song playing on the radio as his mother engaged him in conversation.
He said to his mother, "I am so happy to be going to Anansi."
"Anansi is such a very good man," Mrs. Grace responded.
"But what can he do?" Peter queried. "Is he going to tell me to tell the boys to return my lunch to me?"
"From what I hear, that is not his style." Mrs. Grace responded. "I believe God is going to give him a solution for you so you can eat your lunch in peace without being harassed.
Your visit to Anansi will also gain you a lot of respect and the students will think carefully before

picking on you. Anansi has influence, or should I say, Anansi is influence."

Peter smiled, looking up at his mother in acknowledgment, "I know, Momma."

They travelled on in silence, lost in their own reflections.

The music continued to play.

They were awakened from their thoughts when the bus driver said, "Nansi Stop!"

The bus jerked to a halt in the upscale neighborhood where Anansi lived.

Mrs. Grace and Peter disembarked.

Peter was very excited. He touched Mrs. Grace and ran. Mother ran and caught Peter who slowed to allow her to catch up. She hugged him, and they walked the rest of the way with their hands around each other.

> IT'S WORTH IT TO BE HAPPY
> GO TELL IT TO SOMEBODY
> IT'S WORTH IT TO BE HAPPY
> IT'S WORTH IT
> IT'S WORTH IT TO BE HAPPY
> GO TELL IT TO SOMEBODY
> IT'S WORTH IT TO HAVE A JOYOUS SMILE
> ITS WORTH IT JUST TO LAUGH A WHILE
> IT'S WORTH IT
> TO BE HAPPY - VENECIA (SIS. PRECIOUS) STONE

Peter was in awe when he saw the house of Anansi. "Wow!" he said, placing his hand on his mouth; "magnificent!"

His mother nodded in agreement, sharing his sentiments.

They approached the door and knocked. A servant answered. She was very warm and welcoming.

"I am Mrs. Grace. We have an appointment with Anansi at 9:00am," Mrs. Grace said.

"Mr. Anansi is expecting you," the servant said smiling and ushering them inside.

She brought them into the waiting room and invited

them to sit down.
When they were seated, the servant left the room. Mrs. Grace presumed she had gone to inform Anansi that his guests had arrived.

ANANSI COUNSELS PETER

Anansi entered his dining room, dancing to his theme song, Fifty Dollar Note.

Spend me like the fifty dollar note
Let me be the one You use the most
A currency of heaven
To be spent down here on earth
To be tendered for Your people
Use me Lord

It was obvious that this song motivated him and focused his heart on his mission.

The dining room was a large magnificent place with an antique oval-shaped table. It had an assortment of fruits with a selection of pastries and other delicacies.

Anansi sat down at the table and prayed. "Lord help me to make an impact on Peter today."

The servant returned to Peter and Mrs. Grace at that moment.

She looked at Mrs. Grace warmly and said, "You and Peter will be having breakfast with Mr. Anansi this morning, Mrs. Grace."

Peter and Mrs. Grace looked at each other and Peter knew she was thinking what he was thinking.

"How did Anansi know we had no breakfast this morning? How could he know that we could not afford to have breakfast?"

The servant ushered them into the dining room.

Anansi who was already seated at the table stood up and said, "Come and sit down Peter. Mrs. Grace, I am so delighted to have you eating with me this morning."

Peter and Mrs. Grace sat down and Anansi took his

seat.

Peter looked around. He said in his mind, "This is the first time I have seen so many lovely things in one place. This is the first time I have ever sat at a table with all this food. This is more than I bargained for."

Anansi said to Mrs. Grace and Peter, "Help yourself. I want you to enjoy the hospitality of Anansi today. Eat as much as you desire. Enjoy."
Mrs. Grace and Peter began taking food cautiously, but then they found so many inviting foods, they could not resist.
The servants were at the table taking requests and passing the foods. Some were also seated and eating.

After they began eating, Anansi looked at Peter and said, "So Peter, I hear the bullies are taking away your meals at school. Your God certainly knows how to prepare you a table in the midst of your enemies.
He will certainly continue to provide for you in the presence of all those who make themselves your enemy."
Mrs. Grace licked her lips. The food was tasty but what Anansi said was even tastier to her spirit. She said to herself, "Anansi sure knows how to make an opening statement. He is using this banquet to teach us a lesson of God's provision. To make us know not to give up."

Anansi then turned to Mrs. Grace and said, "There has been some drama at your son's school, Mrs. Grace."
"Oh yes, Mr. Anansi," Mrs. Grace responded. "This set of boys has been causing a lot of trouble. Andrew is in ICU and I hear he may not make it." Her face lost its smile and became sad with concern.
"Mother has been praying for Andrew," Peter added, "and she has been praying for Richard too. Though Richard needs to be punished, we would hate to see him go to jail."

Anansi felt his heart warm towards Peter and

his mother in that moment. "These two have com-passion. Compassion is the key to living a true life," Anansi said to himself. "They have the right hearts. Nothing moves me like people who are compas-sionate. Nothing is more touching than people who can find compassion in the midst of their own dif-ficulties."

Anansi smiled secretly. He answered Mrs. Grace and said, "Andrew will be ok. I got a call from the doctors this morning that he has recovered and is out of ICU. He will be out of the hospital in a few days."

Mrs. Grace's face lit up with a celebratory smile, and she said, "Praise God!" Peter was also visibly very happy.

He said, "God has answered your prayers Mamma!"

"Yes, He has my son," Mrs. Grace said.

There was a brief silence and the two slipped away in happy reflection

Anansi broke the moment of silence and said, "So Peter, I hear you are doing very well in school."

"I try to do my very best, sir," Peter responded.

"I admire you very much because I hear you do it although, many times, you have no dinner...." An-ansi paused then added, "...and no lunch."

Peter said, "Yes sir, the bullies take it away from me, but I work even harder.

My children church leader always says, 'You sacri-fice today to build your future.'

This is his favorite quote, 'You build your dream by sleeping less and working more, not by dreaming more and working less.'"

"Your teacher is very wise," Anansi said. "That statement is so true. That is how Jesus built His kingdom on earth. He did not have a place to lay His head. Sleep was not His priority. In fact, He is quoted as saying, 'I must work the work of God who sent Me to work while there is an opportunity to do so, since seasons change when I will not be able to work.'

There comes a time when only the work that is

completed will have a voice. Jesus was always working on His assignment until it was finished. He understood that time was limited. You see, Peter, Jesus is now in heaven and the dream is spiraling on the foundation He laid through hard work and sacrifice in His time on earth.

The best of life comes through sacrifice Peter. The only thing that can really stop you from achieving your goals is you."

Peter reflected on what Anansi had said until he had finished eating.

Anansi was silent for a while.

Breakfast was finished and Anansi said to Peter, "Peter, I have designed a game just for you, it is called 'Vultures'."

Peter looked excited. "For me sir?" He asked.

"Just for you Peter," Anansi responded. "Let us go into the Anansi Hall."

"Anansi Hall?" Peter repeated.

Anansi smiled, "That is what a child who came to see me named it, and everyone likes that name." Anansi led the way and Peter and his mother followed.

Anansi led them into a beautiful hall decorated as a garden with real flowers and a waterfall.

This was a marvel of home designing. It was also a technical marvel. Anansi could change the decor into whatever 3D design he desired at the push of a button.

Laid out in the middle of the floor was a big real-life game. The characters were real, yet, just characters. The game was a natural landscape with a very beautiful garden, a clear river with a waterfall was in the clearing of a forest. A vulture was perched on a limb in the forest near the clearing.

On the other side of the vulture was a mountain of rock and behind the rock was a dead goat.

Anansi said to Peter, "Your job is to place the vulture where her heart is.

You get to throw the die. If you get any number between two to four you can send the vulture in this

beautiful clearing where it can bask in the sunshine, and enjoy the river and the waterfall.
You just need to press this green button to get there. If you get a six, you press this button that looks like a rock. It will open up the mountain rock. You will need another six to pass through to where the dead goat is.
If you get a one, and the rock is open, it closes again, and you will need to start over."

          "I will throw also," Anansi continued, "If I get two sixes, I can force you into the beautiful meadow or behind the rock. I get to choose for you.
If you have the rock open, and I get a six I can close it. Are you ready?"
The music played.

         THE PRICE OF LAUGHTER WHO CAN PAY
         BRING THE HEART OUT ANY DAY
         WHEN THE HEART GOES OUT TO PLAY
         YOU'VE GOT LAUGH TO GIVE AWAY
         IT'S WORTH IT

Peter threw the die. He got five.
Anansi said, "Peter; you have the option to move into the meadow to where the waterfall is."
"I will pass this time Mr, Anansi," Peter said.
Anansi threw the die. He got a four.
Peter then took the die and threw again. This time he got a six.
He excitedly pressed the rock.
The rock opened and he could see the dead goat.
Anansi threw a six. He pressed the rock button to close the rock.
Peter threw the die. He got a two. He did not move.
          Anansi then said to Peter, "Peter why don't you go into that beautiful meadow with the fruit trees?"
"Because that is not where the vulture's heart is." Peter responded. "It is on the dead goat."
"You are very wise, son," Anansi said. "You are already a master. Let us change the game."

Anansi pressed a button and the game changed. In the place of the vulture was a tiger. He had the green pasture full of green trees and the fall on one side. On the other side, behind the rock, was a herd of deer. In a corner was one weak deer by itself feeding. It had strayed from the herd.

Anansi said to Peter, "This game is similar to the first. Four or five or six gets you through the rock, another four or five gets you to the herd, six gets you to the stray deer.

One, two or three gets you into the meadow with the fruit trees and falls.

Now you must place the hungry tiger where his heart is.

This time you play alone, you have six throws."

Peter threw his die, he got a five.

He quickly pressed the rock and the tiger jumped through.

Peter threw again. The die fell on five once more. Peter did not move.

"Come on," Peter said. "Give me a six!"

Peter threw the die again. It fell on two and Peter did not move.

Peter was anxious as Anansi watched in silence, a big smile on his face.

"Come on now," Peter said

He threw again. The die fell on six. Peter jumped.

He quickly placed the tiger where the single isolated deer was feeding by itself.

The game lighted up with lights running up and down and all around it and the room was filled with the announcement, "Winner, winner; we have a winner!" Confetti came down from overhead on Peter's head.

A package came out of the machine.

"Take it Peter." Anansi said. Peter, looking mesmer-ized took the package and opened it. It was a gift voucher to the central bookstore in town. It was enough to purchase school books for the entire school year, next year.

Peter thanked Anansi and handed it to his mother.

The feeling was exhilarating.

"You got it perfect, Peter." Anansi said. "Why did you choose the isolated deer?"

"It was easy picking," Peter responded. "It was all by itself, isolated. It was a guaranteed meal for the tiger."

Anansi said to Peter approvingly, "You got them both correct, Peter. The tiger will select the easy prey. It isolates and then, it kills.

Is it possible that the bullies pick on you because you are isolated?"

"I don't have many friends," Peter said.

"It is very good to have good friends at school," Anansi responded.

"Friends can be very mean," Peter said, "And many times they are involved in things that God says are wrong."

"True," Anansi said, listening to Peter's heart.

"My children church leader says bad company will corrupt my manners," Peter said.

"That too is very wise, Peter," Anansi said. "That means you have to choose your company carefully. I know just the right person. Have you met John?"

"You mean Bi..." Peter was about to say Big Nose, but he caught himself. "Yes, I know John," he answered.

"He is such a new person lately. I would love to be his friend."

"Well go and introduce yourself Peter," Anansi said, "And tell him, I say hello."

Anansi then said to Peter, "Do you remember our game of vultures Peter?" Peter nodded.

"The lessons from the game of vultures will be the solution to your situation," Anansi said.

"You are very intelligent Peter. You played to win. You also understood the heart of the game from the start. The heart of the vulture will always go after the dead animal.

Jesus used this truth to teach a lesson also. He said, 'Where dead meat is the vultures will gather togeth-

er.'
If you understand the hearts of the bullies you will be able to outsmart them and to have your table prepared in the presence of your enemies."
"Understand their hearts?" Peter said, questioningly,
"Yes," Anansi said. "Just as you understood the heart of the vulture and the tiger, you can understand their hearts.
The bullies are after your food. They are rewarded for their bullying by your food. They enjoy it so they keep coming back.
They are also rewarded by your fear. It makes them feel powerful and respected."
Peter nodded. He was silent for a while and then, he began smiling from ear to ear.
"What is in your heart Peter?" Anansi said. "How would you play your hand?"
"If the goat was alive, the vulture would not be interested," Peter said. "They cannot kill it, and they cannot eat it alive."
"What if I make the food very peppery or salty?" Peter said in his thoughts.
He could see in his mind's eye the bullies spitting out the lunch and running for the bathroom. He envisioned all the children laughing.
Peter chuckled as Anansi studied him. Peter said aloud, "O no! I can't do that." He was still smiling as he rebuked himself.
"What were you thinking Peter?" Anansi asked.
"I cannot tell you sir," Peter said.
Anansi then said to Peter in a stern almost scolding voice, "You were not thinking about putting something bad on the food, were you Peter?"
Peter looked ashamed as he nodded.
"This never works, Peter," Anansi said. "It will only make the bully angry, and he will want to get back at you. Even if he withdraws, you would have lost because you would have become a bully yourself. You would have made him a laughing stock.
Jesus says, you do not overcome evil with evil, you

overcome evil with good.

The Bible tells us to be kind and affectionate to each other, to love them like brothers and to place their preference above ours.

You are also commanded to do to others as you would have them do to you.

Do you like to be embarrassed before the entire school? Do you like to have people laugh at you?"

Peter was silent for a minute as what Anansi was saying slowly sank in.

Anansi waited on Peter. After a moment's silence, Peter spoke up softly, "No sir. I hate embarrassment."

Anansi then said to Peter, "It is so easy and normal for us to do to others what we would hate others to do to us. To make happen to others what we would hate to happen to us. So many people are guilty of this. Jesus says to do the opposite."

Anansi pressed a button, and fire sprung up in a small fire place. It looked as if it would blaze up and get out of control.

Anansi said to Peter, "Peter, do you see those two sealed cans. I want you to take the one you believe is the right one and put that fire out."

Peter looked at the cans, one was labeled fire, the other water.

Peter got up and selected the sealed can marked water. It was very light, he shook it.

"This is surprisingly light for water," Peter said to himself.

He was about to open the can and Anansi said, "Do not open it yet Peter!"

Anansi pressed a button and the fire went out.

"Excellent selection Peter," Anansi said, congratulating him. "You cannot put out fire with fire, all you get is a bigger blaze. You have to take the opposite approach.

There is something in that can that will help you and your mother. You may open it when you leave. Peter, to get the vultures to stop haunting you, this is

what you must do."
Anansi continued speaking as he gave Peter instructions.
Peter nodded his head. He smiled. His mother was smiling also. She was nodding her head.

The song Fifty Dollar Note played softly. Anansi was finished. The time was rich and well spent. Peter felt that he had many years added to his life in that session with Anansi. He felt he was so much richer and wiser.

"Goodbye Peter," Anansi said. "Thank you for bringing Peter, Mrs. Grace."
"Thank you oh so much Mr. Anansi," Mrs. Grace responded to Anansi.
"Thank you Sir. I am so very grateful," Peter said to Anansi also.

Peter and his mother stepped through the door.
"Peter, are you forgetting something?" Anansi said, calling after Peter.
Anansi points to the can labeled water.
"Oh, oh!" Peter said. "I would hate to have left that."
"You certainly would," Anansi said. "You may open the can when you get home. And remember, there is always a good reward for taking the right approach."

Peter hugged his mother as they headed home.
"This is so precious Mamma," Peter said. Tears of joy and satisfaction were in his eyes.
Peter and mother returned home in silence. They hugged each other on the bus as the song Love Will Pick You Out played on the radio.

At the door of the house, Peter handed the can labeled water to his mother. Anansi had said to open it when he reached home. He wanted his mother to open it.
"Open it, Mamma, please!" Peter said.
Mrs. Grace opened the can. In it was a stash of large notes. It was full of money.
At the top of the can was a note to Mrs. Grace from

Anansi. It was written in his own unique handwriting.

It read:

Dear Mrs. Grace. God desires to favor you and to end your struggles.

Peter and Mrs. Grace danced and cried and laughed spontaneously.

The African beat of the song, GOD'S HANDS echoed in her mind as she danced.

> WHEN YOU SEE GOD'S HAND
> IT'S NEVER EMPTY
> HIS HANDS ARE NEVER DRY
> THIS IS YOUR SEASONS OF THE PLENTY
> IT'S GOT THE RAIN INSIDE
> IF YOU CAN SEE THE NAIL SCARS IN HIS HANDS
> YOU'VE GOT ETERNAL LIFE
> WHEN YOU SEE GOD'S HAND IT'S NEVER EMPTY
> HIS HANDS ARE NEVER DRY
>
> GOD'S HANDS - CLIVE WARREN

Mrs. Grace broke down in tears and worshipped. She said in prayer, "Anansi can never know how much this means to us; he cannot; how can he? This is all you God. The glory belongs to you! Continue to bless Anansi and keep his heart doing good works."

Peter thought of a passage he learnt in Sunday School, "Let your light so shine before others, so they will see your good works and give glory to God who is in heaven."

When Peter was alone, he repeated in his head over and over again every minute detail of his session with Anansi.

God had prepared them a table in the middle of their time of adversity.

He remembered the illustrations:

The tiger chooses the isolated deer.

The vultures are after dead meat.

Fire cannot extinguish fire, overcome evil with good.

The most precious thing to Peter, however, was the instructions Anansi had given him to deal with the bullies. He could not wait to get back to school.

85

1. THE POWER BELONGS TO YOU. IF YOU ARE BEING BULLIED, PLEASE REMEMBER, THE POWER BELONGS TO YOU!

2. EVERY HEART HAS A NEED AND EVERY BULLY HAS A CREED; YOU CAN GIVE BULLIES A WINLESS WIN IF YOU UNDERSTAND THEM.

SONIA AND THE SEXUAL BULLIES

It was afternoon. Sonia and her father, Mr. Rhema sat in the garden outside their home. It was a small modest home set in a beautiful landscape. The garden was well tended and tantalizingly attractive.

Father hugged Sonia. The song TAKE IT TO THE SKIES echoed in his head.

> I'VE BEEN WATCHING YOU MY DARLING
> AND I HAVE SEEN YOU GROW
> BIT BY BIT THE GENIUS IN YOU
> HAS BEGUN TO SHOW
> YOU HAVE BEEN CREATIVE
> AND I HAVE BEEN AMAZED
> AND AS I GAZED INTO YOUR CREATIVE MIND
> I SHOWERED YOU WITH PRAISE
>
> NOW I'M HERE TO SEE YOU
> PUT YOUR ART ON DISPLAY
> IT'S LIKE WHEN I WATCHED YOU DANCING
> ON THAT VERY FIRST DAY
> YOU RUN TO ME FOR YOUR HUG
> AND I GAVE YOU A KISS
> AND REAFFIRMED TO YOU MY LOVE
> AND SOFTLY WHISPERED THIS
>
> TAKE IT TO THE SKIES MY BABY
> TAKE IT TO THE WORLD
> LET THEM KNOW YOU'VE GOT IT IN YOU
> RIDE HIGH MY LITTLE GIRL
> TAKE IT TO THE SKIES MY BABY
> RIDE AMONG THE STARS
> YOU CAN DO ANYTHING
> ANYTHING YOU WANT

Mr. Rhema squeezed Sonia and said, "I am so proud of you. You are exceptional. You have not betrayed your faith in spite of the pressure."

"It is very difficult daddy," Sonia sighed. "These girls are pressuring me to surrender my purity. They do everything you can imagine.
But I remember what you say, 'I do not belong to myself. I was purchased with a price. I am not my own. Jesus owns me. I am not free to do with my body what I desire.'"
"Thanks for remembering, my daughter," Mr. Rhema replied. "You are very special. Only the owner can determine what to do with his property. You are not free to give yourself away."
"I know, daddy," Sonia said. "That is why I have resisted them and maintained my focus. Have you seen my latest class report?"
       Sonia handed him her class report. As her father opened it she said in an excited voice, "Surprise!"
Mr. Rhema looked at the report and jumped in excitement. He hugged Sonia and they danced happily. Sonia had excelled to the top of her class once more.
Mr. Rhema sang to Sonia.

I KNOW EVERYTHING YOU DO
IS GONNA TO BE A GRAND SUCCESS
YOU HAVE NOTHING AVERAGE IN YOU
YOU'RE BETTER THAN THE BEST
DON'T LET IT STOP WITH THESE AWARDS
JESUS CHRIST IS YOUR REWARD
DANCE ON THE MOON, RIDE ON THE STARS
UNTO THE PLEASING OF THE LORD

DILIGENT IN ALL YOUR WAYS
BEFORE KINGS YOU SHALL STAND
THE LORD ABOVE WILL BE YOUR PAY
HE WILL MAKE YOU STRONG
UPON HIS SHOULDERS LIFTED HIGH
BY EXCELLENCE YOU ARE DEFINED
LIKE THE SUN HE MAKES YOU SHINE
SO TAKE IT TO THE SKIES

TAKE IT TO THE SKIES - CLIVE WARREN

ANANSI VISITS SONIA

Daddy looked at Sonia. A deceptive smile graced the corner of his lips. It was clear he had something up his sleeve too.

"I have a surprise for you also Sonia," he said.

"Show me Daddy, show me!" Sonia said excitedly.

Mr. Rhema shook his head and said, "Patience Sonia. It will be worth it."

Sonia responded to her father, mocking a sad face, pleading, "Daddy!"

"Do not worry Sonia, he will be here in fifteen minutes!" Mr. Rhema said, almost giving his hand away.

"He?" Sonia said, showing genuine surprise.

Mr. Rhema would say nothing more, therefore, Sonia paced the garden impatiently. Her usual interaction with her special flowers in bloom was lost in the moment.

Anansi was traveling along the road in his personalized horse driven carriage. He loved the beautiful countryside scenery.

Everyone looked out to see him and they constantly greeted him. Anansi was the greatest celebrity to them all. He was not just a celebrity but a perfect example of Christ.

Anansi turned off the road into a private property. It was the property that belonged to Mr. Rhema.

"Daddy!" Sonia said in a voice that mimicked scolding. She turned towards him as she said this, unable to take the suspense anymore.

It was then that Sonia saw the carriage coming in the driveway. She gulped. Sonia held her hand over her mouth in disbelief and said in quiet reverence: "Anansi!"

She turned and hugged her father, jumping excitedly.

"Daddy no! Oh daddy!" Sonia said, not sure how to respond. "I don't believe it! Wow!
It is Anansi! A personal visit. O my God!"

> LOVE WILL PICK YOU OUT
> ON THE GLOBE
> AMONG THE MILLIONS WITH YOU
> IT FINDS YOUR SOUL
> IT WILL AMAZE YOU HOW STRAIGHT IT GOES
> AND ANYWHERE YOU ARE AROUND THE WORLD
> LOVE WILL PICK YOU OUT

"Anansi insisted on coming," Mr. Rhema said to her. "He wants to honor you because of your personal commitment to honor God with your purity."
Tears streamed from Sonia's face as she said once more, quietly "Wow!"

> 1. THERE IS NOTHING YOU DO TO HONOR GOD ON EARTH THAT IS NOT TREASURED AND VALUED GREATLY IN HEAVEN

ANANSI COUNSELS SONIA

Anansi pulled into the parking lot with his carriage and stepped down. The song 'Fifty Dollar Note' played softly and sweetly from his carriage.

A CURRENCY DON'T DICTATE
HOW IT SHOULD BE USED
THE ONE WHO SHOULD RECEIVE IT
OR WHAT IT IS USED TO DO
IT DOES NOT TELL ITS OWNER
WHERE IT WANTS TO GO
AND EVEN SO MY MASTER
I SUBMIT MYSELF TO YOU

SPEND ME LIKE THE FIFTY DOLLAR NOTE
LET ME BE THE ONE YOU USE THE MOST
A CURRENCY OF HEAVEN
TO BE SPENT DOWN HERE ON EARTH
TO BE TENDERED BY THE PEOPLE
USE ME LORD

Anansi greeted Mr. Rhema with a firm handshake. "How are you Mr. Rhema?" he asked.

Without waiting for a response, he said, "Soniaaaaa!" His voice was warm and homely as if he knew her for some time. "Come give Anaaaansi a hug!" he said.

Sonia timidly and with respect went to Anansi and hugged him passionately.

Anansi gave her a warm fatherly hug, then turned again to Mr. Rhema who was saying, "I am so happy you could make it, Mr. Anansi!"

"Nothing pleases me more than coming here to meet a courageous young lady like Sonia," Anansi said. "The pleasure is all mine."

"You have a beautiful home Sonia," Anansi

said, looking around. His attention was solely on Sonia now.

Anansi looked at the garden in full bloom. "And your garden, wow, it is so beautiful!"

"Mother loves gardening," Sonia responded. "She has helped me to plant and tend my very own."

"This is the perfect place for God to plant a perfect flower," Anansi said.

"I like them too," Sonia answered. "I love them very much."

Anansi, looking directly at Sonia, said, "I am talking about you Sonia.

Just as you love and tend this garden everyday, the Lord loves and tends you every day. He thinks about you a whole lot. He rejoices over you with singing."

Anansi is known to use everything at hand for practical illustrations. He was about to use the beauty of Sonia's garden to motivate her.

"How would you like someone to come and trample up and down in your garden and to violate the plants?" Anansi said.

"I would hate that; it would make me mad, very mad," Sonia said.

"This is how God feels when someone violates His garden...your body," Anansi said.

"You would never give anyone permission to trample this garden, would you?"

"O no. Never!" Sonia said firmly.

"What if it was someone else's garden? Your mother's? Your father's? A stranger? Would you feel the same?"

Sonia responded thoughtfully but firmly, "It would be just the same. I would be upset."

Anansi then said to Sonia, "That is why I am so proud you have maintained your purity.

Just as you would not allow anyone to trample your property that you value, you cannot allow anyone to violate God's property that you steward, your body."

Anansi paused, then said, "And it is ok to get angry

to see what others do to their own bodies. It is a natural reaction."

There was silence for a minute. Sonia glanced at her father from the corner of her eyes. He was nodding to everything Anansi was saying.

"Do you like cars, Sonia?" Anansi continued. Anansi had learnt about Sonia's passion for cars from her father so he already knew the answer.

"Oh yes, I love cars," Sonia responded.

"Some cars are rather beautiful," Anansi said. "I own a few, but I always prefer my carriage."

"I always look at the spanking, new cars on the lot," Sonia said, "I love to see the different makes and models."

"Do you know the moment a new car is driven off the lot it loses thirty percent of its value?" Anansi said.

"No sir, I did not know that," Sonia responded.

"That is true," Anansi reaffirmed. "The moment a new car is driven from the lot, it becomes used. Now that is not bad if it is purchased by someone who is willing to pay the full price for it; someone who actually values it. It takes care of that person and that person takes care of it."

Sonia nodded her head. "I will really take care of my first car when I get big and own one," she said.

"But what if it is stolen off the lot by someone who does not really value it?" Anansi said.

"Someone who only wants to use it or to cash in on its value," he continued. "It gets wrecked, it is used in hiding only, it is abandoned, it is even scrapped and sold as parts to cover up the theft."

"Wow!" Sonia said.

"What are you thinking?" Anansi asked, recognizing that Sonia was catching on.

Sonia covered up her body unconsciously, "My body!" she responded.

"Yes!" Anansi responded. "That is just what happens when a girl gives her body away. It is stolen from the lot of the true owner, God. Her body depreciates immediately, and she can never regain her

true purity and novelty."
There was silence for a minute.
"But for the grace of Jesus who makes all things new," Anansi said in reflection. Sonia nodded her head, understanding.

"By the decree of God, every heavenly covenant is sealed in blood. This is the same for the old covenant with Moses and the children of Israel and the new covenant sealed by the blood of Jesus Christ." Anansi said.
"And Sonia, this is why God placed the hymen in a woman to seal the covenant of marriage.

This is the price that is to be paid when a car is driven off the lot. Commitment, love, marriage, care, honor.
You take care of the buyer, the buyer takes care of you.
Sonia, this is why so many women are used, abused, rejected, scrapped, abandoned, you name it. They allow themselves to be stolen from God's lot; to be driven off the lot without the price." Anansi continued.
"And Sonia, the moment you give your purity away, you can never ever regain it."
Sonia and Mr. Rhema nodded. The analogy that Anansi drew was so deep and very real.

Anansi then said to Sonia, "Sonia, the next time those immoral girls tease you about your purity, this is what you are to tell them."
Sonia acknowledged what Anansi was saying by nodding continuously and smiling. Her father was nodding too.
Sonia jumped and hopped when Anansi had finished instructing her. Her hands were in the air and she laughed in excitement.

My darling
My baby girl
Come and kiss your daddy
Then go conquer the world

TAKE IT TO THE SKIES MY BABY
TAKE IT TO THE WORLD
LET THEM KNOW YOU'VE GOT IT IN YOU
RIDE HIGH MY LITTLE GIRL
TAKE IT TO THE SKIES MY BABY
RIDE AMONG THE STARS
YOU CAN DO ANYTHING
ANYTHING YOU WANT
YOU CAN DO ANYTHING
YOU CAN DO ANYTHING

Anansi hugged Sonia then shook Mr. Rhema's hand.

"Thank you oh so much, Mr. Anansi," Mr, Rhema said. A tear was in his eye and a sincere look of deep gratitude on his face. I can never appreciate you enough for this.

"Just keep on raising this beautiful rose for God and that is enough," Anansi said.

Anansi gave Sonia a beautiful gold ring.

"For me?" Sonia asked. "All for you," Anansi said. "Just make me this promise that you will not allow your car to be driven off the lot without the proper price."

Tears were in her eyes as Sonia said, "I promise." Anansi placed the ring on Sonia's marriage finger. "This is a token of your promise. Anyone ask you about it tell them it is your purity ring. A token of your promise to God. The only person qualified to replace it is the person willing to take you off your Daddy's lot at the right price."

TAKE IT TO THE SKIES MY BABY
TAKE IT TO THE WORLD
LET THEM KNOW YOU'VE GOT IT IN YOU
RIDE HIGH MY LITTLE GIRL
TAKE IT TO THE SKIES MY BABY
RIDE AMONG THE STARS
YOU CAN DO ANYTHING
ANYTHING YOU WANT

You can do anything
You can do anything

Take it to the skies
My little baby girl
Let these words remain with you
When I'm with you no more

Anansi hugged Sonia again, then he got up into his carriage and drove off.
The song Fifty Dollar Note lingered as he left.

Spend me like the fifty dollar note
Let me be the one You use the most
A currency of heaven
To be spent down here on earth
To be tendered by the people
Use me Lord

> 2. NORMAL IS DEFINED BY THE DICTATES OF THE MANUFACTURER. IT IS NORMAL TO BE PURE IT IS ABNORMAL TO BE PROMISCUOUS.
> 3. YOU CAN HIDE FROM THE TRUTH BUT IT WILL FIND YOU WHERE YOU ARE: MODERN TRADITIONS, CHANGING CULTURE, COMPROMISING NEW LAWS, LOWERING MORAL STANDARDS, DO NOT STOP THE ARROW OF TRUTH POINTING AT YOUR HEART.
> 4. BECAUSE IT IS ACCEPTED, AND BECAUSE IT IS POPULAR, DOES NOT MAKE IT RIGHT.
> 5. CHICKENS CANNOT FLY WHERE EAGLES GO; INSTEAD THEY LOOK UP AND TREMBLE. NEVER BE PRESSURED TO LOWER YOUR STANDARDS.

BOOK THREE

ANANSI MEETS THE BULLIES

CHAPTERS IN BOOK 3

ANANSI'S HOSPITAL VISIT

The school bell rang for the close of school. Richard went to the gym to exercise. He had to keep fit for his sporting activities.

Andrew sat in his classroom after class. This was his first day back to school after his horrifying ordeal. His classmates were patting him on the back, giving him their support.

Mr. Gideon, his class teacher walked into the classroom. He smiled when he saw Andrew.

Mr. Gideon came up to Andrew and said, "What you did with Richard is very courageous and amazing. You could have sent him to jail, yet, you opted to pardon him."

"That is what Jesus would want me to do," Andrew said.

Nodding his head in acknowledgment, Mr. Gideon continued, "Did you see how many students cried when the principal announced to the school how you chose to forgive that bully. You could have died."

"It is not just me," Andrew said, "Anansi came to visit me at the hospital when I came out of ICU."

"Anansi," Mr. Gideon said with surprise and interest showing in his voice.

"Yes Anansi," Andrew said, glowing. "That was the best day of my life."

Andrew began to visualize the moment Anansi walked into the hospital.

The song, Love will pick You out, was playing in Andrew's head as Anansi came into the general area of the hospital.

Andrew was surprised at first to see the local hero in the hospital, but surprise quickly turned to awe and then disbelief as Anansi came up to him and stopped at his bedside.

All the staff and patients stopped what they were

doing and had their eyes fixed on Anansi.
Andrew's heart leapt as Anansi looked into his eyes
and said, "Hello Andrew. How are you doing today
my son?"
Andrew's voice was bright as he responded, "I
am doing so much better, Mr. Anansi. I was told I
would be out of here by tomorrow."
"I had no doubt you would recover quickly," Anansi
said to him, "I prayed for you."
"Thank you so much Mr. Anansi," Andrew said. "I
would never have known."
"Let me tell you something Andrew," Anansi continued, "you can get better physically, but if you get bitter inside, you would have left here worse than how
you came in.
How do you feel when you think about Richard and
the others who did this to you?"
        Andrew remembered gritting his teeth as he
responded, "Angry, very angry. If I could I would
repay them in kind; every one of them."
"That would be your greatest disaster," Anansi
quickly corrected Andrew.
"I want you to picture Jesus on the cross. Everyone
was bullying Him like a pack of hungry wolves.
They spat on Him, pushed Him boxed Him, placed
thorns on His head to prick Him, mocked Him to
add insult to this injury and teased Him to come
down from the cross.
If He had come down in response to them, He
would have reduced Himself to their level and they
would have eaten Him. He stayed pure and clean
so He could pull them up to His level.
        Andrew, why do you think He said, 'Father
forgive them?'"
"Because they did not fully realize what they were
doing?" Andrew said.
"Yes," Anansi said, "but also, He did not want them
to contaminate Him. If He had not forgiven them,
He would have gone down to their level, He would
have given them the only true victory they could
have. A bully never truly wins unless you give them

the victory; you have to permit them to steal your joy."

Anansi handed Andrew a decorated stick looking like a staff.

"Hold on to this staff, Andrew," Anansi said. "I want you to hold it with all the feelings, all the passion, all the hurt, all the anger you feel towards Richard and the bullies."

Andrew held on to the staff with a very firm grip. Some people in the hospital had drawn closer to observe.

Andrew gripped the staff very tightly with his hand held a little distant from his body as Anansi instructed. A point like a spear came out and began to grow slowly. The harder Andrew gripped the spear, the faster it projected, although still very slow. The longer Andrew held the staff, the closer it inched towards his chest.

Realizing the danger, Andrew released the staff quickly and the point went back in. Then out sprang the most beautiful rose Andrew had ever seen.

Anansi chuckled as he looked at Andrew and said, "If you hold on to anger and hurt, it becomes a dagger aiming at your heart. The longer you hold it, the larger and more dangerous it becomes. It possesses you and destroys your life.

If you let it go, it releases you and becomes a positive force that can bloom in yours and the other person's life.

This spear would not have harmed you, it is built with the necessary safeguards including a soft rubber tip which looks metal in appearance only. Hurt has no power to hold you, but it can control and possess you if you hold onto it. That is why God commands us to forgive."

Anansi gave the staff to Andrew, and he walked out to the cheers of the onlookers. Andrew felt special. He was reminded of the words of the song Love will Pick you Out.

Andrew was aware of the look of amazement

on Mr. Gideon's and his classmates' faces as he told his tale.

"That is why I hold nothing against Richard," he said, "it was easy to forgive him. I did it for myself."

"And for him too," Mr. Gideon said cheering. All the other persons in the room followed Mr. Gideon's lead and began cheering also.

"Richard was released on probation," Mr. Gideon said. "His life has not been the same since."

One of the students in the class, Ravi, entered the conversation. "Yes, Richard is so very different now. He has withdrawn from his crowd of bullies."

"He studies hard, he goes to church, and he is very serious about his life," teacher added. "If he continues on this path, he will be an A student very soon."

"He is on the football team also," Ravi said. "He trains very hard. I believe he is at the gym as we speak."

CHANGE. CHANGE,
YOU CAN HAVE IT IF YOU WANT IT:
WALKING IN THE PATH OF DESTRUCTION
REMOVE YOUR FOOT FROM EVERY EVIL WAY
YOU WILL NOT FALL INTO CORRUPTION
HE'S BUILDING YOU LIKE BLOCKS EVERY DAY
KNOW THAT YOU ARE UNDER CONSTRUCTION
AND IF YOU WILL DO WHAT HE SAYS
GIVE YOUR EARS TO HIS INSTRUCTIONS
LEANING ON THE LORD THERE IS CHANGE

Andrew's heart was filled with a warm sensation as he listened to the progress Richard had made. Tears of joy came to his eyes as he thought, "I would have gotten it so wrong if I had chosen not to forgive."

"Richard is my friend now," Ravi said.

"He will be mine too," Andrew said, "but I am worried for him. I hear the bullies are planning to harm him."

"God will keep him safe," Mr. Gideon said. "I prayed for him."

Andrew did not tell anyone what he did with that rod. He kept it safe as his most precious possession. He caresses it and dusts it every day. Andrew is yet to find out just how valuable it is. He will one day discover the diamond button is real, it is worth thousands.

6. UNFORGIVENESS IS MORE DISASTROUS AND DE-STRUCTIVE THAN THE ORIGINAL ACT OF SIN AGAINST YOU.

7. A PERSON MAY HARM YOU BY THEIR ACTION, BUT YOU USE THEIR ACTION AS A DAGGER TO INFLICT WOUNDS TO YOURSELF OVER AND OVER AGAIN, LONG AFTER THEY HAVE MOVED ON, BY REFUSING TO LET GO.

8. TODAY IS A GOOD DAY TO LET GO OF THE SELF-INFLICTING DAGGERS OTHERS HAVE BUILT FOR YOU - LET GO AND LIVE!

THE BULLIES REGROUP

The atmosphere was ominous as the bullies met in the foyer of the gym. They were after one of their own who defected, Richard. They wanted to punish him.

"We cannot touch Andrew now," Donald said, "Everyone would have our heads. He has become so popular!"

"Let us teach Richard a lesson. Nobody gets up and walks away that easily."

Alex responded with an evil laugh, "Ha, ha. We will make him wish he was still in prison."

The rain was still falling outside as the bullies walked into the gym.

Richard was lying down on an exercise bench lifting weights.

"There is Richard," Andy said. The group of boys made their way over to him and stood on both sides of the bench he was lying on.

Alex held onto one side of the weight bar Richard had lifted in the air and Andy held the other side. Richard was afraid to let it go and have it fall on his chest so he held on still.

"Do you find our weight too heavy for you to bear?" Donald asked. "Well try this."

The bullies let the weight bar go but quickly held it again as it sunk Richard's weary hands.

Richard began speaking, His voice strained under the burden of the weight he held. "What you are doing is wrong man. We must change." His voice was measured and strained.

"Change?" Donald said. "What change? We love things just the way they are!"

Change, change,
You can have it if you want it

> CHANGE, CHANGE OH, OH,
> TALKING BOUT CHANGE
> WALKING IN THE PATH OF DESTRUCTION
> REMOVE YOUR FOOT FROM EVERY EVIL WAY
> YOU WILL NOT FALL INTO CORRUPTION
> HE'S BUILDING YOU LIKE BLOCKS EVERY DAY
> KNOW THAT YOU ARE UNDER CONSTRUCTION
> AND IF YOU WILL DO WHAT HE SAYS
> GIVE YOUR EARS TO HIS INSTRUCTIONS
> LEANING ON THE LORD THERE IS CHANGE

Richard, seeing that they clearly intended to harm him, tried to appeal to their senses. "Please man, don't do this!"

"If you do not change and get back with us you will be begging very soon," Donald said. "It is going to get very serious."

Just then a bat flew near Donald's head. He did not tell anyone before, but he was afraid of bats. Donald shifted his head showing the fear he would normally keep hidden.

In making his move, Donald accidentally touched the hand of Andy who was holding the weight on his side. Unknown to them all, the pins were taken out of the bar carelessly to change the weights and not replaced as the other user had to leave in a hurry.

One of the weights fell off the bar and onto Andy's foot. He was holding the bar over Richard. Donald was on the other side. The other weight followed suit. Andy screamed, "Ooooowie, ooooouch!"

He immediately let the bar go in a hurry without thinking. The bar tilted and the weights fell on the feet of Donald on the other side of the bench.

Donald could not suppress the pain. He swore aloud and cursed. He immediately bolted or rather, hopped through the door and took off in the rain. The other bullies retreated after him. Andy was visibly hurt and whimpering.

Richard said to himself relieved, "God certainly knows how to deliver. He has such a great sense of

humor."
A student who was watching from a distance began laughing uncontrollably.

Donald was nursing his wounds at the school
garage nearby. The bullies went over to him.
"Look at this now," Alex said. "How can this happen
when tomorrow is my big day?"
"Big day?" Donald said, groaning slightly from the
pain in his foot. "What are you talking about Alex?"
"O you forget Donald," Alex responded. "Tomorrow
is my first date with Sonia."
"Oh, Sonia!" Donald responded. Recognition entered
his voice.
"The girls are on her case. I heard that the last time
they pestered her they had her in tears."
"I know," Alex said. "I just love it. They are going to
totally blow her apart at the game tomorrow and I
will be present to let her know when it happens, I
will always be there before the next teardrop falls.
She will never guess that I am the cause of her pain
and tears."
The bullies laughed together and the sound was
sinister.

"Sonia is a tough case," Donald said. "She has
been very resolute but the girls know their job. They
tell me the walls of Jericho will come down tomorrow."
Donald laughed, patting Alex on his back, "I will be
there to watch it happen and to support you bro."
"I even bought some hair-do to give me some extra
curls for the occasion," Alex said.
Donald laughed again, then grimaced as he tried to
shift his weight forgetting about the sore foot.

The rain stopped. The boys began to walk
home.
"Kem seems very confused these days," Donald
lamented.
Bill entered the conversation. He had joined the
group recently and was usually very quiet and calculated.
"He hangs out with us sometimes, but he is not his

usual self," Bill said.

"We must not let up on Peter," Donald said. "I love that home cooked lunch."

"I will handle Peter," Bill said

"So what do we do about Kem, Bill?" Alex questioned.

"I heard he has promised to get counsel from Anansi in exchange for not getting persecuted," Bill responded.

"That is dangerous man," Alex said. "No one has been to Anansi and not changed."

"Let us go with him to keep him straight," Andy suggested.

"Good idea!" Donald responded. "We cannot afford to lose another one of our own."

"We will take on Anansi as a team,"
 Bill said enjoying the idea.

The boys then separated and headed for their individual homes.

> THERE IS NOTHING MORE FULFILLING, NOTHING MORE INSPIRING, NOTHING MORE ASSURING, THAN KNOWING YOUR HEART IS IN THE RIGHT PLACE

SONIA'S BUBBLE

It was morning.
Sonia woke up to the sound of the rooster's crowing in the backyard. The golden glow of the morning sun was streaming through her bedroom window. It kissed her with a kiss of pure warmth on her cheeks. She opened her eyes and smiled.
Sonia opened her window and was greeted by another of nature's delights. The gentle brush of the morning breeze caressed her face. It brought with it the smell of the morning.
"Nothing beats the perfume of the blossoms," Sonia said breathing it in. She loved it. She was in love with her day. She was in love with life. She was in love with Jesus who created the day.

Sonia went to the bathroom and refreshed herself, then ran down to the kitchen where her mother was already putting breakfast on the table. Sonia hugged her mother and father. She was happy.
She was in love with her parents. She was bubbly. They were a close knit family who loved each other dearly.
She went to the cabinets for plates and immediately began to help.
The oneness of her family made it easy for her to honor God who she saw everyday in her parents, but she was convinced she would have honored Him either way. She was very disciplined in studying her Bible and she was in love with prayer. The Word of God made life worth living for her.

Her mother noticed her energy. "You have been so happy since you met with Anansi," her mother said.
"I am Mamma," Sonia said with a satisfied smile on her face. "It is like all my problems have disappeared and life is so much better living pure. It is as if I would have been such a loser if I had yielded to

the temptation to give in. I can't believe I even allowed these immoral girls to get close to me; to disturb my peace. And Momma, I love this ring Anansi gave me. It reminds me of such a great story, the real and only truth. I belong to Jesus….and also to you Daddy!" She added laughing turning the most beautiful and innocent face his direction.

They sat at the table to eat and Mr. Rhema prayed. "Lord, I thank you for this food. We consider it a blessing since we know so many others are in need. Continue to bless us, but make us a blessing so we may bless others like Anansi does."
As Mr. Rhema finished, Sonia reached across the table and squeezed Mr. Rhema's hand. "Daddy, I cannot thank you enough," Sonia said.
"You make me so proud to be a father," Mr. Rhema said sincerely. "Go and take it to the skies my daughter."

TAKE IT TO THE SKIES MY BABY
TAKE IT TO THE WORLD
LET THEM KNOW YOU'VE GOT IT IN YOU
RIDE HIGH MY LITTLE GIRL
TAKE IT TO THE SKIES MY BABY
RIDE AMONG THE STARS
YOU CAN DO ANYTHING
ANYTHING YOU WANT

"Our school has a netball game today, and I will be there to see us get to the finals," Sonia said.
"Tell me all about it when you get home," Mr. Rhema said.
Sonia did not realize in that moment how much would unfold that day, and the intriguing turn of events she would have to report.

They finished eating and Sonia got ready. She hugged her father and mother and left for school. She walked past the beautiful garden, interacted with her flowers and headed through the gate. Sonia loved her garden before, but now, since Anansi visited it, she loved it even more. Sonia loved life.

She would never surrender any of this. Now she was even more resolved, she would not surrender her body. She knew it would rob her of her joy completely. She could not trade her dignity for cheap pleasure and the myriad of problems that comes with it.

1. *BULLYING IS AN ACT OF HOSTILITY AND HATRED. A PERSON WHO DOES NOT LOVE DOES NOT KNOW GOD FOR GOD IS LOVE.*
2. *YOU LIE TO YOURSELF WHEN: YOU PUT AN EAGLE UNDER WATER AND TELL IT TO SWIM; YOU PUT A WHALE IN THE AIR AND TELL IT TO FLY; YOU BECOME A BULLY AND EXPECT LASTING SUCCESS.*

ANANSI CONSULTS WITH DEEP INFORMATION ON BULLYING

Anansi was in his study early that morning. In fact he was up long before daybreak. His interaction with the many persons being bullied had troubled him. There were so many children being bullied. There were so many children bullying others. They could not see the massive problem they had.

He had prayed for a long time.

After praying, Anansi felt the need to get some information on bullies. He knew that knowledge was his basis of functioning—the knowledge that came from available information and the knowledge that came from the Holy Spirit. Anansi believed he had to study to show himself approved. He needed to study the Word of God and get the wisdom available on the topics he addressed. He would then depend on the Holy Spirit to direct his moments.

Anansi consulted with his mechanical companion, his interactive computer, Deep.

"My people perish because of a lack of knowledge," Anansi said. "They reject knowledge. I will not reject knowledge. I will embrace knowledge. I will dance with knowledge."

Anansi danced into the mechanical arms of Deep and pressed the button as the tune NOT ENOUGH MOMENTS played.

Deep woke up and responded to Anansi with its own shake that resembled a dance.

Deep then spoke to Anansi,

"At your service, your resource
You just speak and I will surf."

"Tell me all you know about bullying, Deep," Anansi said.

The lights flashed on the screen as it began surfing.
Deep then opened its mouth and responded to Anansi with a mechanical voice. It spoke in its usual
rhythmic style:

> Well there is physical bullying
> This is the one everybody sees
> When someone bigger, stronger and more aggressive
> takes set on someone who is weak.
> They may hit them, shove them, kick them
> And abuse them physically
> This is physical bullying
> But it is not all there is;

Deep was putting on a performance, dancing and
swaying as it spoke.
Examples were flashing on its clear screen.

> Then you have verbal bullying
> Where by insults and name calling they de-
> mean
> They choose their targets based on
> The way they look, act, or their personalities
> Very often they attack children who appear
> weak
> Children with special needs
> Many adults feel that words cannot harm,
> But the emotional scars are deep and real.

> Then there is relational or emotional bullying
> It is sneaky, insidious and easily missed
> It is social manipulation where one tries to hurt
> or sabotage the social standing of somebody
> else
> Relational bullies often ostracize others from
> a group, spread rumors, manipulate situations
> and demoralize.
> These bullies use this method to increase their
> own social standing.

It is usually done more frequently by girls,
called mean girls or frenemies
But it also exists at workplaces
And in other types of relationships

Then comes cyber bullying
Where one harasses, threatens or embarrasses
someone else
Using the internet, a cell phone or other tech
to say things they are afraid to speak face to
face.

Sexual bullying is also on the list
This is where someone uses harmful
and humiliating actions to target a person
sexually
This includes sexual name-calling, crude
comments,
vulgar gestures, uninvited touch.
They use sexual propositioning and
pornographic materials
Slut shaming, sexting and other such the like
to target another sexually
This has led to assault many times.

Prejudicial bullying is based on prejudices
Race, religion or sexual orientation.
This type of bullying is severe
And can open the door to crime from there.

So why do bullies bully?
Some say and may be right
The Bully Has Been Bullied Before
The Bully Is Lonely
The Bully Has Problems at Home
The Bully Has Low Self-Esteem
The Bully Is Jealous
The Bully Is Part of a Pack
The Bully Has a Big Ego
The Bully Likes to Impress
The Bully Sees You as Being Different

But why do bullies bully?
Control is top of the list
To exert dominance
To have power over others
To make themselves important by this
These bullies can be impulsive, hot-headed
They love to be able to subdue and to
distress others.

Next on the list of reasons is reward
They love the positive reinforcement they get
Material rewards, the things they steal
Next is the status, attention, fear and prestige
And they bully also to increase popularity.

Bullies have a common trait
They lack empathy and they enjoy other
people's pain
They are also unable to self-regulate
Family backgrounds have a role to play
Studies have come to this conclusion
That bullies come from families
with little warmth and small affection.

Anansi listened and absorbed all the information
Deep gave to him. He knew the information would
come in handy if he was to effectively address the
serious problem of bullying.

KEM MEETS WITH DONALD

"**H**ey Kem," Donald said, shouting at him from a distance. Kem saw Donald and came over to meet with him.

"Hello Donald," Kem said, touching hands with him. Donald placed his hand firmly on Kem's shoulder and said, "What's up bro. Your heart has not been with us of late."

"I have been thinking a lot lately," Kem responded. "This thing with Andrew shook me up."

"But why?" Donald said. "Don't you see that even Richard has gotten away free."

"You know the truth man," Kem said. "It is only because Andrew begged for him.

Do you know the only reason I was not arrested is because I promised to change and take counseling?"

"I did hear you are planning to go see Anansi," Donald said.

"Oh sure," Kem said. "The arrangement is already made for tomorrow."

Looking at Donald sheepishly, Kem continued, "I don't know what this will mean for us, but whatever happens, I love you bro."

"Don't worry, everything will be ok," Donald said. "We are going with you."

"What!" Kem responded surprised. "I am not so sure about this. Daddy already made arrangements to come with me."

"Listen man," Donald said, "You reschedule, make the arrangements. However, you do it, do it!"

"That is not so easy man," Kem responded immediately, alarmed. "I don't even believe it is possible. We are talking about Anansi. He is very busy."

"That is your problem Kem, do it!" Donald asserted and walked off.

SONIA STRIKES BACK

It was afternoon. The school was abuzz. The children had been dismissed early to facilitate the big netball game.
The stands were almost full as this match was a final. Sonia wanted to be there to support her team from Champion High School. As she walked she hummed:

> TAKE IT TO THE SKIES MY BABY
> TAKE IT TO THE WORLD
> LET THEM KNOW YOU'VE GOT IT IN YOU
> RIDE HIGH MY LITTLE GIRL
> TAKE IT TO THE SKIES MY BABY
> RIDE AMONG THE STARS
> YOU CAN DO ANYTHING
> ANYTHING YOU WANT

Sonia was very excited as she made her way to the game. She walked by Rose who was standing on the side of the road talking. Rose was a classmate who had shown some empathy for Sonia.
"Hello Rose," Sonia said.
Rose looked up at her and smiled. Sonia returned the smile.
Rose laughed to herself as Sonia smiled, "She thinks I am her friend, ha, ha! Just a pity she does not know what is waiting for her at the game."
Rose waved goodbye to Sonia, still smiling. "See you at the games," she said deceptively.
Sonia waved goodbye to her.
        At that point Rose saw the ring on her finger and said, "What's up with that ring on your finger?"
"It is my purity ring. Anansi gave it to me," Sonia said.
Immediate concern showed on the face of Rose.

"Is something wrong?" Sonia asked.

Rose realizing she was giving herself away, began smiling once again. "Oh no!" Rose said, "at least you have got someone now," she said sarcastically.

"No.. not like that..." Sonia responded.

But Rose was off without giving Sonia a chance to finish or to explain.

Rose wiped the smile from her face the moment she left Sonia and concern returned. "Sonia has been to Anansi. I must warn Lavern and the others," she said.

Sonia went into the stands and sat down beside a cluster of the supporters of Champion High. Sharon, Lavern, Sandra and a group of other girls came and sat down beside her on either side.

Some other girls moved, seemingly innocently, and made way for them.

Donald, Alex, Andy and some of their gang of bullies came and sat down behind her.

Rose was seated in the stands some distance to their left. She looked up and saw Lavern and the others with Sonia.

"Oh, no!" Rose said to herself, louder than she wanted to. "How am I going to tell them she has been to Anansi? This will not be as easy as they imagine."

The game was moving at a fast pace and Champion School was losing, 14:25.

Lavern looked behind her and acknowledged Donald. Donald nodded and winked at her.

This was the cue Lavern needed to begin teasing Sonia. Their team was losing anyway so they would at least have some fun.

Lavern began talking across Sonia to Sandra on the other side of her. "Hello Sandra," Lavern said, "what do you do with old pails?"

"You throw them out," Sandra responded.

"And what do you do with old maids?" Lavern continued.

"You laugh them out!" Sandra said.

Sonia had caught on immediately. This was the group of girls who derided her because of her virginity.

Everyone was laughing. The girls, the boys behind her and others also. Alex appeared to be concerned but secretly he was having fun also.

Sonia blushed but kept silent. She looked behind her, and she saw Alex.

Alex made a face as if showing concern, but he did nothing. He was pretending.

Sonia looked away. Alex laughed silently.

A drop of tear graced Sonia's eye as she made this song her prayer:

> WHEN THIS WEARY WARRIOR IS WOUNDED IN THE FIELD
> LET THE ANGELS UP IN HEAVEN SEND UP PRAISES
> JUST FOR ME
> AROUND THE THRONE OF GLORY
> WHERE ONE DAY I WILL BE
> FROM THE THRONE OF HEAVEN
> SING FOR ME
>
> FROM THE THRONE OF HEAVEN
> SING FOR ME, SING FOR ME
> FROM THE THRONE OF HEAVEN
> SING FOR ME
> SATURATE MY HEART, WITH HEAVEN'S SYMPHONY
> FROM THE THRONE OF HEAVEN
> SING FOR ME

Sharon then took over with a chant of her own:
> "Take my money out my pocket
> Take the food off my plate
> Takes a fool to have never ever been on a date."

Sandra chipped in. They intended to break Sonia this time:
> "You don't know what you're missing
> You don't know just what is cool
> Life begins in the boy's lane
> What a waste for a fool."

A teacher sitting near the group began to get concerned.

Rose from her position tried to indicate to the group to be careful. She shook her head to say no, but Lavern ignored her. She could not decipher her communication.

Lavern continued her harassment of Sonia:
"Cannot take the heat
Then get out of the kitchen
Go and find a BF
And you will find what you are missing
In this day and age
Say you are still a virgin
You are the biggest joke
See everybody laughing."

All the girls laughed. They laughed so hard and others all around joined in.

Sonia blushed:

TEMPTATIONS, PERSECUTIONS, OR ANYTHING I MEET
ON THIS JOURNEY FOR MY KING AND I'VE DONE
EVERYTHING IN ME
YOU WILL FIND ME STANDING BUT MY REQUEST WILL BE
FROM THE THRONE OF HEAVEN
SING FOR ME

FROM THE THRONE OF HEAVEN
SING FOR ME, SING FOR ME
FROM THE THRONE OF HEAVEN
SING FOR ME
SATURATE MY HEART, WITH HEAVEN'S SYMPHONY
FROM THE THRONE OF HEAVEN
SING FOR ME

Lavern continued:
"Cannot take the heat
Then get out of the kitchen
Go and find a BF
And you will find what you are..."

Sonia would take no more. She was calm to this point.

Sonia got up and shouted above the noise of the game, "Stoooop!"
The stands were silent; everyone in the stands on this side was looking at her.
At that moment Sonia remembered her meeting with Anansi very vividly.
The silence was the perfect pitch for a flash back. She could hear her father's voice, "Anansi insisted on coming. He wanted to honor you because of your personal commitment to honor God with your purity."

She could hear the voice of Anansi, filled with care and godly wisdom, "How would you like someone to come and trample up and down in your garden and violate the plants?"
Sonia replayed her response, "I would hate that; it would make me mad, very mad!"
Anansi's response lived with her, "This is how God feels when someone violates His garden…your body."
Anansi had continued, "You would never give any-one permission to trample this garden, would you?"
"Oh, no! Never," Sonia had said emphatically.
Anansi had asked her then, "What if it was some-ones else's garden? Your mother's? Your father's? A stranger?"
"It would be just the same. I would be upset." So-nia heard herself saying, just as she had responded then.
The words Anansi spoke in response came sooth-ingly to her heart inspiring confidence. He had said, "I am so proud you have maintained your purity. Just as you would not allow anyone to trample your property that you value you cannot allow anyone to violate God's property that you steward, your body. And it is ok to get angry to see what others do to their own bodies."

Her heart warmed for what she was about to do as she remembered what Anansi said about new cars, "Do you know the moment a new car is driven off the lot it loses thirty percent of its value?" "No, I did not know that," Sonia had responded. "That is true," Anansi said, "The moment a car is driven off the lot it becomes used.

And that is not bad if it is purchased by someone who is willing to pay the full price for it; someone who actually values it. It takes care of that person and that person takes care of it."

"But what if it is stolen off the lot by someone who does not really value it?" Anansi had said.

"It gets wrecked, it is used in hiding only, abandoned, even scrapped and sold as parts to cover up the theft."

This was the moment Sonia had realized the futility of immoral living. She had covered her body unconsciously.

She could hear the voice of Anansi coming to her with clarity. Saying so truthfully, "This is what happens when a girl gives her body away. It is stolen from the lot of the true owner, God. Her value as pure and preserved depreciates immediately, and she would never regain her true purity and novelty."

Then his advice came. He had said, "Sonia, the next time those immoral girls tease you about your purity, this is what you are to tell them..." Sonia remembered the song that played on that memorable day:

> TAKE IT TO THE SKIES MY BABY
> TAKE IT TO THE WORLD
> LET THEM KNOW YOU'VE GOT IT IN YOU
> RIDE HIGH MY LITTLE GIRL
> TAKE IT TO THE SKIES MY BABY
> RIDE AMONG THE STARS
> YOU CAN DO ANYTHING
> ANYTHING YOU WANT
>
> TAKE IT TO THE SKIES

MY LITTLE BABY GIRL
LET THESE WORDS REMAIN WITH YOU
WHEN I'M WITH YOU NO MORE

She was about to do just that, to take it to the skies.

Sonia looked at her ring and smiled. She brimmed with confidence, conscious of all the eyes looking at her, waiting for her to fall apart, to meltdown. She was about to do exactly what Anansi told her to do, and she was savouring it.

Spacing her word for effect, Sonia said, "Any day I want..."
Sonia paused for a few seconds recognizing that she had her audience.
"Any day I want," Sonia repeated, "I can become like you..."

TAKE IT TO THE SKIES MY BABY
TAKE IT TO THE WORLD
LET THEM KNOW YOU'VE GOT IT IN YOU
RIDE HIGH MY LITTLE GIRL

Sonia then drove her message home, "You can never, ever, ever become like me."

TAKE IT TO THE SKIES MY BABY
RIDE AMONG THE STARS
YOU CAN DO ANYTHING
ANYTHING YOU WANT

The jaws of Lavern and the other girls dropped.
They looked down, afraid to look around.
The teacher sitting nearby rose up from her seat and began to clap.
Everyone in the stands rose up and clapped.
Alex and Donald quietly slipped away.
The bullying girls were on the opposite side of the attention. The reality of what Sonia had said was sinking in.
They began trying to cover themselves up. They were feeling a little dirty and cheap.
For the first time their promiscuous lifestyle was re-

121

vealed for what it truly is, dirty.

Then the attention of everyone quickly turned to the game as the supporters of Champion School began shouting.

The Champion team seemingly inspired by the cheers from the spectators lifted their game and was leading 51:49.

The game was blown off and Champion won.

After the game, one of the players explained to a friend what had inspired them to win. "We were losing," she explained, "until our supporters began to cheer. We lifted our game. We could not disappoint this confidence in us."

Her friend laughed, "The cheers were for Sonia. She lifted her game beyond the clouds. The rain of her showers just fell on you. Your performance capped off a perfect day of courage and determination."

Rose caught up with Lavern, Sandra and the others as they tried to slip away before the others.

"I was trying to tell you that she has been to Anansi," Rose said.

"So why didn't you?" Sharon asked, "you could have saved us this embarrassment."

"I tried, I really did try."

"The tables have turned on us," Sharon said.

"Yes," Sandra agreed. "Now, it feels dirty and cheap to be so involved...you know what I mean."

Sharon and Lavern looked down and said, "Yes, Sonia is right. Immorality is nothing to boast about. Sonia has a strong point."

There was extended silence as the girls slipped into their own individual reflection. It felt good to have everyone celebrate them and their immoral lifestyles. It felt terrible to be so exposed before the entire school.

1. IT IS GAME ON WHEN YOUR ENEMIES THINK YOU ARE GAME, NOT REALIZING, YOU HAVE NOT YET PLAYED YOUR BEST GAME
2. IT IS ALWAYS EASY TO CLUCK WITH THE CHICKENS, BUT CHICKENS CANNOT IGNORE THE GRACE AND NATURAL FORCE OF AN EAGLE!
3. IF IT DOES NOT HAVE A FOUNDATION IN GOD'S WORD, IF IT CANNOT MEET WITH GOD'S APPROVAL, THEN IT IS NOT YOUR STRENGTH BUT YOUR GREATEST WEAKNESS FOOLING YOU!

KEM VISITS ANANSI

The day was partly cloudy as Kem and his father set out in his car to visit Anansi.

The beautiful country road held a mesmerizing allure against the grey skies. Kem had always enjoyed traversing the country roads. This was something he did not have to own or control or bully to enjoy. He loved nature in its many shapes, shade, and colors.

"I am very proud to have you for a son Kem," his father, Papa Samuels said to him as they drove. He was careful to reaffirm his love for Kem so Kem could be confident when he met Anansi.

"I have not told you how disappointed your mother and I have been with your behavior," Papa Samuels continued. "Your mother often cries in the night because of you. Now she is so happy you have made the decision to change."

"I am so sorry Papa," Kem replied.

Everyone called his father Papa. He was a well-loved man. "I tried to ensure you did not find out."

At this his father paused and sought wisdom.

"If we don't know, Kem, it does not make it right," his father reprimanded him. "It only makes it more hurtful. We have tried so hard to raise you right!"

"I know, Daddy," Kem said. "But you are hardly there, and it really felt so good to have the respect of the group I run with. These guys command the respect of everyone."

"But it almost landed you in prison Kem," Papa Samuels said. "There are consequences for every action. And then, why do you need to steal, taking away another child's lunch?"

"It felt bad at first Papa. I did it for the crowd but after a while, it felt very good. And the food was getting better. Peter's mother can cook."

"Kem!" His father said in a voice of surprise mixed with disappointment and reprimand.

"But I am sorry. It is so wrong," Kem corrected himself.

Just then, the car made a funny noise and began wobbling.

Kem's father stopped the car and exited to check.

"Punctured tire," he said to Kem, who was exiting the car from the other door. "Now we are going to be late."

"Let me help you Papa," Kem said. Then with a voice of concern, he added, "Are we really going to be late?"

"If we hurry we may make it just about on time," Papa Samuels responded.

"I do not want to be late, Papa" Kem said.

"Neither do I," Papa Samuels responded.

Kem and his father worked hard and quickly changed the tire. They both entered the car and began driving again.

"You know Donald?" Kem asked.

"Which Donald?" Mr. Samuels responded. "The leader of the bullies," Kem said. "Well, he wanted to come with me to Anansi. In fact, he insisted that I take him."

"But that would not be possible," Papa Samuels said.

"I told him," Kem replied, "but he insisted that I should make it happen."

"But why?" Kem's father queried.

"I believe he wants to sabotage the meeting," Kem responded, "or at least to be there so he can dissuade me after."

"Let us tell it to Anansi," Papa Samuels said, "he will know how to deal with Donald."

"Look," Kem said. "Anansi's house. I heard so much about it. I could pick it out anywhere."

---

4. IF YOU LIVE A DOUBLE LIFE, WHERE YOU HAVE SOME THINGS TO HIDE, AND YOU LIE TO KEEP IT HIDDEN; THEN LYING BECOMES LIVING, INDEED YOU LIVE A LIE.

5. THE DEVIL IS THE LIAR AND THE DECEIVER; SILENCE THE DEVIL, REJECT HIS CHARACTER

ANANSI COUNSELS KEM

Papa Samuels pulled his car up on the sidewalk in front of Anansi's driveway. He was just on time.

As Papa Samuels opened his door and stepped out of the car, a man grabbed his wallet, bounced him to the floor and ran.

Kem jumped out of the car and started running after the thief. It was futile. He had too great a head start and he was too fast.

Kem returned to his father, and said, "Are you ok daddy?"

Mr. Samuels looked distraught. "I am ok," he said, "I have just a slight bruise."

He then said in a voice filled with concern, "Oh no! That wallet contains all my important documents. What am I to do now?"

"We won't let him get away with it," Kem said. "That thief must learn his lesson. Let us call the police."

Just then, the servants of Anansi came running out.

They held the hand of Papa Samuels gently and asked, "Are you ok sir?"

"I am fine," Papa Samuels said. "Thank you, oh so much!"

"Let me look at that bruise," a very pleasant servant said. She was about middle aged. "I know you have been mugged. Anansi will know what to do."

She bent down and examined Papa Samuel's foot, then said, "it seems ok. Just a scrape. Let me get you a band-aid."

At that moment another servant came out to the front. He looked at Papa Samuels and said, "Are you Mr. Samuels?"

"Yes, I am," he responded.

There was something vaguely familiar about this young man. It was his shape, his walk, mannerism. Both Kem and his father knew they met him before, but they could not place him.

"Come on in," the servant said. "Anansi is waiting on you."

Papa Samuels and Kem were brought around the house to a beautiful secluded garden at the back near a swimming pool.

Anansi was already seated reading a book. Papa Samuels noticed how casual he was. He felt it strange that he was so casual about what just occurred at his gate, but he said nothing. The very presence of Anansi pushed the incident to the back of his mind.

A humming bird that was busy with a flower nearby moved to another flower. There was a bee in that flower.

The bee refused to budge as if to say, "I got here first."

The bird shoved the bee with its beak very hard, as if to say, "Yes, but now I am here. Give way!"

The bird then opened its beak wide. This time definitely suggesting, "Next time you go inside."

The bee dejectedly flew away.

"What in the world is wrong with bullies?" Kem who was observing found himself saying.

Mr. Anansi rose up to greet them, "Good morning Kem."

Kem stuttered, "Hello Mr. Anansi. Thanks so very much for having me."

Anansi then turned to Kem's father, "How are you today, Mr. Samuels?"

"It is a good day, and I am happy to be here," Mr. Samuels replied. "But, I had two bad experiences today. First, I got a puncture and then I was just robbed at your gate."

Anansi responded with a grimace. His face held a deceptive half smile mixed with what appeared to be concern. "My gate!" he responded smiling.

"Yes sir," Papa Samuels said. "The thief took all my

important documents."

"Don't worry about it. You will get back your documents," Anansi asserted as if he had the situation under control.

Kem and Mr. Samuels looked at each other.

Anansi sure had something up his sleeve. Perhaps, he was just making his usual dramatic introduction.

"Tell me what happened, Mr Samuels," Anansi said.

"As I got out of the car at your gate," Mr. Samuels said, "someone came by, shoved me and took my wallet.

It happened so quickly. I fell to the ground, and he was gone.

Your servants were so gracious to offer a hand, but I lost all my documents."

Kem grimaced unconsciously at the thought of his father's pain.

Just then, Anansi's servant came and offered drinks to everyone.

"Kem," Anansi said, "how do you feel about your father being mugged?"

"I feel very terrible and angry," Kem said. "That thief deserves to be in prison for a long time!"

"Why do you feel that way?" Anansi asked.

"Because he is a thief, Mr. Anansi," Kem responded. "He does not know how much he has disturbed my father's life. He could have seriously harmed him. O my God!"

"That is so true," Anansi said calmly.

"He does not know how hard my father has to work to get the money he has stolen," Ken continued.

"That is so true," Anansi said again, calmly studying Kem.

"If I had caught him, I would have taught him a big lesson and after that I would hand him over to the police for him to rot in jail."

"Do you feel this strongly about all thieves?" Anansi responded.

"Of course," Kem said, "And I have all rights to. You

cannot take what does not belong to you just like that and expect nothing to happen."

"You are right," Anansi agreed with Kem, "The Bible commands us not to steal.

Do you know what it is to covet?"

"Yes sir," Kem replied. "It means to desire to have something that belongs to another person."

"Do you know Kem," Anansi said, "You have to covet before you commit the crime of stealing?"

"I hate covetous people!" Kem said.

"Do you really?" Anansi asked.

"Yes sir, with all my heart," Kem responded. "I hate thieves. I want to see every one of them in jail.

"Do you really feel this strongly about thieves?" Anansi asked again.

"Yes sir, I surely do," Kem said.

"Even those who steal the lunch of other children?" Anansi asked.

At this question, the silence became deafening. Kem was stunned. He realized he had just cornered himself.

Kem paused. He stuttered a bit of nonsense, "Well ahh, well..." Kem then hung his head in silence and shame.

Anansi waited for Kem to regain his composure.

After a while, Kem said, "I am sorry sir. I can see what everyone else is doing, but I am never looking at myself.

I do deserve to be in jail too, don't I?"

"You do," Anansi said. "But you have a good heart. I saw you clench your fist as you watched the bee being bullied. The bee and the bird are artificial and programmed.

In every bully, there is the potential to change."

Kem was distracted as he saw the bird carrying the bee on its back. It took it back to the petal. The humming bird then touched the bee gently with its beak as if to say, "I am so sorry to have bullied you. I will respect you in the future."

The bee rubbed against the bird as if to say, "You have such a perfect heart!"

The humming bird stepped back with a look of guilt, as if to say, "Even after what I have done?" Kem could hear the audible sound. It appeared to be coming from the bee. The voice said, "It is what you do in the end that matters."

Kem realized he was watching a cartoon production on a screen that blended perfectly with the garden.

Anansi was still looking, waiting on Kem who was still recovering from the shock of realizing he had just condemned himself.

Anansi said to Kem. "Kem, it is what you do in the end that matters. How do you intend to fix the problem you have created?"

Kem thought for a minute, then said, "I will invite Peter to have lunch with me and I will take lunch for him some days."

"You have a very good heart, Kem," Anansi replied. "Please remember, stealing starts with covetousness. Giving is the opposite of coveting. Jesus says it is better to give than to receive."

Anansi then pointed to his garden, still addressing Kem. "Do you see that flower over there?"

"It is beautiful!" Kem responded.

"Do you like it?" Anansi asked. "O yes, I really do," Kem said.

"It is the prettiest flower in my garden," Anansi said. "You may have it. Go ahead and pick it."

Kem went and picked the flower which was in full bloom.

"I will keep it forever," Kem said.

"Is that true?" Anansi said. "It will not survive for more than a few days with the best of care, then it is dead, and you will throw it into the garbage."

Kem nodded his head in acknowledgment.

"This is what happens when people go for glory," Anansi said. "And especially when they do so at the expense of others. They pick their flower. Their glory will last only for a short time and then...everything falls apart, the leaves begin to fade. They may even end up in jail.

Jesus says that anyone who exalts themselves shall be brought down. But if you humble yourself, He will exalt you.

That flower in your hand is glorious, but when it is picked it has a quick end. It soon withers, just like the glory of bullying.

The fate of that flower is a reminder of the type of glory you get by bullying.

All these flowers that are left on the plant will live much longer than this pretty one that is picked. No one will be disappointed when they all die a natural death, Kem. But if you like this flower you pick, you will be disappointed when it dies. Ensure that you keep your life founded on sure principles. Work hard for everything you have. Never go for glory that is not earned. Never pick your glory before the time."

Anansi then turned to Papa Samuels who was listening and observing quietly nearby and said, "So Mr. Samuels did you get a good look at the person who stole your wallet?"

"No, I did not," Papa Samuels said. "He had on a blue top with a green pants, but I did not see his face. I was certainly not expecting this at your gate."

"Jeffery," Anansi called.

One of Anansi's servants came running. He was the same servant who had ushered Kem and his father to Anansi. Papa Samuels realized immediately where he knew him from. He would recognize the run any day. It was the person who had stolen his wallet.

"Please, return Mr. Samuels' wallet to him," Anansi instructed.

Jeffery returned the wallet and Mr. Samuels smiled. Anansi then said to Papa Samuels, "Mr. Samuels, thanks for cooperating for this object lesson. We did not warn you of the nature. We do apologize for Jeffery being so rough and for the bruise.

No one steals at Anansi's gate," he said laughing. Realization came upon the face of Papa Samuels immediately, then he broke out into a big smile. "Oh my, that was it!" He said. "Ha, ha. It was my pleasure to participate."

Anansi then said to Kem, "This mugging was staged, but mugging happens everyday. I am happy you have become true to your real self, that you have discovered the good in you."
"Thank you oh so much sir," Kem said.

Kem then said to Anansi, "Mr. Anansi, Donald the leader of the bullies wanted to come with me today. I did not bring him, but he will not take no for an answer. I do not believe his intentions are good. Could you still see him?"
Anansi responded, "I will. Tell him and all the other bullies with him to come to me on Thursday at 3:00pm"
"Thank you, sir," Kem said.

Anansi led Kem and Mr. Samuels into his orchard, there was a great assortment of fruit trees fully fruited. "You may pick all the fruits you want," Anansi said.
Kem pointed to a big fruit looking rosy red in color. It was large and inviting.
"What fruit is that?" Kem inquired.
"It is a very unique fruit from Asia. There is no other like it here in this country," Anansi replied.
"Can I try this one?" Kem asked.
"Oh sure Kem. Go ahead and taste it," Anansi said. Everyone is always tricked by this fruit. Anansi knew it was the best looking but worst tasting.
Kem took a big bite into the fruit, then, he quickly spat it out and distorted his face miserably.
"This is really awful," Kem complained. "It has a very funny taste."
"It does," Anansi said, "it is best for juicing."
"You see Kem," Anansi continued. "It is not what appears rosy on the outside that is truly rosy, but it is what is rosy on the inside that is truly rosy.
You may go ahead and pick the fruits you desire to

take home."

"I better stick to the fruits I know," Kem said to himself laughing as he took up Anansi on his offer.

Kem walked past the tree with the rosy fruit and began picking fruits from the trees he was comfortable with.

Anansi allowed him to pick as many as he desired. The servants brought a box to put the fruits in.

Anansi walked Kem and his father to their car. He said to Kem then, "Kem, I see you picked the fruits you knew to be good and tasty."

"Yes sir," Kem said. "I stuck with what I know this time."

"I noticed you avoided the tree you ate from," Anansi said. "What do you have to say about that tree, was it a good tree or a bad tree?"

"It was definitely a bad tree," Kem said.

"You are perfectly right," Anansi said. "You see Kem, Jesus says a good tree bears good fruits.

The fruits looked very good on the outside, but it was terrible inside.

This is how bullying is. It looks attractive on the outside. It appears cool, and powerful and rewarding, but inside, at the very heart, it is wicked and detestable to both God and man. The fruits of bullying and the life of a bully cannot be digested."

"Oh! Oh!" Kem exclaimed.

"You must bear fruits Kem, so you can be palatable to others, not just look good on the outside," Anansi said. "Bear fruits of truth, and honesty, and honor, and integrity, and kindness, and generosity.

Live the way you want to be remembered when you die.

No one wants people to speak about how wicked they were, how oppressive, or how unjust."

"No sir," Kem agreed.

"When a person dies, the eulogy only speaks about the good part, Kem; the integrity, the generosity and how amicable they were. The other part that is bad is omitted."

There was a brief silence as Kem reflected on

what he heard, "Thank you sir," he said under his breath. "Thank you oh so much sir."

"My car! The tire is repaired and it is changed!" Mr. Samuels exclaimed with surprise.

"Jeffery wanted to do you this favour," Anansi said. Anansi then turned to Kem and said, "Jeffery does not want to be remembered for how rough he was to your father, but for his kindness and his good heart.

How do you want to be remembered Kem? Today is always a good day to begin to make it right and to change the records!"

Kem and his father left Anansi. They felt fulfilled as they drove back home.

"That was so refreshing," Papa Samuels said as he turned into his driveway.

"It really was," Kem said. His eyes were wet.

> 1. COULD YOU APPRECIATE EVERYTHING YOU DO IF THE THINGS YOU DO WERE HAPPENING TO YOU? IF THE ANSWER IS NO, YOU CANNOT! THEN YOU WILL APPRECIATE THAT YOU SHOULD STOP.
> 2. DO TO OTHERS AS YOU WOULD LIKE OTHERS TO DO TO YOU. NEVER FEEL AT HOME DOING BAD THINGS TO OTHERS, BECAUSE, WHAT YOU DO TO OTHERS WILL FIND ITS WAY HOME.

PETER TURNS THE TABLE

Peter walked to school with Jeff. He was excited. Life for them both was so different now.

"I enjoyed the lunch you brought for me yesterday Peter," Jeff said, "that was so tasty. Your mother can really cook."

"No denying it," Peter agreed. "She has got that special touch Jeff."

"You better be careful Peter," Jeff said. "Bill saw you give me the lunch, and he was eying you. I believe he is up to something."

"That is just what I want him to do, Jeff," Peter said. "Anansi has prepared me to deal with him."

"Anansi, wow!" Jeff said. "I would love to help, is there anything I can do?"

"No, Jeff. They have too much respect for you since you went to Anansi. You may spoil the fun," Peter said. Then he said reflectively, "Well, there may be…"

Peter smiled as he whispered instructions to Jeff. "What a great idea," Jeff responded laughing. "I really do not know why everyone scorns Cran so much. They say he is nasty."

"He is always picking his nose, and he refuses to wash his hands," Peter said. "He boasts that he puts cockroaches in his sandwiches for extra protein."

"I don't believe he really does this. I think he is just bragging for attention," Jeff said.

"I don't know man," Peter said. "I would not want to take that chance. No one at school would take the chance."

Peter whispered something to Jeff and he reacted very surprised. "You have done what!"

"Yes," Peter said, "I have arranged with Cran to take his lunch today in exchange for mine.

I want to see the look on the bullies' faces when they find out what they are eating."

At school that day, Peter was impatient. He could not wait for lunch time to come. He wanted to carry out his plan. He was relieved when the bell rang for lunch break.

Peter sat at his desk with the lunch on the table. Most of the students had left the classroom.

It was not long before the bullies came streaming through the door. A cold shadow entered the room with them that brought a sense of foreboding. A few of the students close to the door quickly exited. Some of the others were too afraid to leave. They did not want to be targeted.

Peter was sitting at his desk with his lunch on the table.

Donald came and sat down in front of Peter. Alex sat behind him. The other bullies were standing nearby.

Peter's friend, Jeff, was watching from a distance. Bill came up to Peter. He was the main player assigned to Peter.

Bill placed his hand on Peter's desk and knocked. He said, "I see the rat has no time to hide his cheese today."

Peter was silent and apprehensive. Those who did not know he had a plan would perhaps think he was fearful.

"I know what you did the last time," Bill said. "You hid your lunch from us."

Bill picked up the lunch on the table and opened the wrapping.

The word Cran that was written on the disposable carrying bag he threw in the garbage became visible.

Bill and the others did not see it.

Bill said to Peter sternly, "Don't you ever play that card on us twice. You will regret it."

"Hello Donald," Bill said, reverting the conversation to his leader. "Kem has been telling me, this boy's mamma can cook."

"We are going to make her our chef for life," Donald said, laughing.

Alex joined in then, "And Peter is going to be our waiter."

Bill sank his teeth into the sandwich. "He will bring the food to us at school and serve it with a smile."

Peter, remembering the games with Anansi smiled to himself.

"The raven's heart is on the dead meat. Well, this one is live, very live!" he said to himself.

Speaking up for the first time, Peter reacted with a show of extreme concern. "Oh no!" he said.

The bullies laughed at the thought that he was in misery. This reaction of fear, anger or pain was the icing on the cake for them.

Jeff, watching from a distance was breaking up with laughter. He had to hide his face in his hands.

Peter turned the tables with his next words. "Oh no!" he said. "That is Cran's lunch! See the paper you threw into the garbage."

The name Cran was visible on the top of the wrapping Bill had thrown into the garbage.

Bill's face immediately reflected nausea as he quickly spat out the lunch he had in his mouth.

He immediately dropped the rest of the lunch on the floor. He then acted as though he was going to vomit.

By this time the entire class was laughing. Everyone had forgotten their fears and laughed uncontrollably at Bill's humorous reaction.

The other bullies could not help it, they were laughing uncontrollably also.

Peter said to Bill as if trying to save the situation.

"Don't worry, Bill. There are no roaches in this one. At least, I can't see any!"

He had so much control as he spoke, but the laughter increased with his humor.

"I know you must be hungry to take Cran's lunch. You may have my lunch.

My mother did prepare an extra one for you today. She says if you were not hungry, you would not steal."

This embarrassed the bullies as it exposed

them as weak and vulnerable, which was opposite to the image they projected.

Bill seemingly embarrassed, still with that nauseating look, was grateful for the act of kindness. He responded in a subdued voice, "No man, thank you. I can't eat anything for the rest of the day after this."

"I am going to wash my mouth with soap. I can imagine the insects crawling around inside me now!"

The laughter was thunderous.

John walked over and shook Peter's hand as if they were long time great friends.

The bullies looked on and quickly retreated.

Bill's face was filled with misery as he exited.

As they entered the school yard, Bill rushed to the pipe and washed his mouth repeatedly as if he was paranoid.

The bullies laughed throughout his entire ordeal. Someone threw Cran's lunch outside but missed the garbage bin. It bounced back and fell at Bill's feet.

He stepped away from the pipe and into Cran's lunch. When Bill saw it he jumped and screamed and the bullies laughed uncontrollably.

Donald said to his group, "We laughed at this, but this is very serious."

"We are beginning to look like fools," Alex said. "This is not just Bill, it is all of us."

Just then the school bell rang and Donald said, "Let us meet after school to discuss this. Usual place."

After school, the bullies met at the playground.

"I don't know what Peter was doing with Cran's lunch," Donald said, "I bet it was a set-up. Do you want us to teach Peter a physical lesson?"

"No man," Bill said. "Peter was kind in the end and while everyone was laughing, including all of you, real buddies, he was the only one to reach out to me."

"I don't care!" Donald said angrily. "We cannot have Peter taking over our space and making all of us look bad. What will the other children do when they hear this?"

"Donald is right," Andy said. "Did you see how close Peter and John appear to be?" Alex said.

Donald said in reflection, "Yes!"

"If they are really good friends," Alex said, "We must be very careful. John is very popular now. People are beginning to like to see the Big Nose around. If we touch Peter, and he is a friend of John, it may backfire on us. It will be even worse for our reputation than eating Cran's food."

Kem was just walking up. He heard the conversation and said, "It seems Peter has gone to Anansi too."

"What!" Donald said, then checked himself in acknowledgment. "I should have known. That is why Peter and John seem to be such good friends." Donald then said in anger, "Anansieee! No! You are messing up my profile Anansi."

"I went to Anansi," Kem said. "It was extremely good! I even got you an appointment for tomorrow."

"Don't make fun of us man," Donald said. "We were supposed to go with you.

We don't care about Anansi's counsel. We wanted to be there to defeat it. To ensure he does not infect you with his smart poison too."

Alex seemed to ignore what Donald was saying. He expressed his own thoughts, "An appointment with Anansi. Yes!"

"After a day like this, I need that," Bill said, picking up on the thoughts of Alex. "I will be there!"

"I bet Anansi has gotten into you too Kem," Donald said, ignoring them. "I am not going anywhere. Who is Anansi anyway? He is a greater troublemaker than I am."

"Do you think people truly respect you, Donald?" Kem said.

"Well…" Donald said thoughtfully. "At least they fear me, and I force them to show respect."

"What do you think they say about you behind your back?" Kem asked.

"I don't think about that. Why should I think about that?" Donald said impatiently.

"Because you know the truth," Kem continued.

"Who needs truth?" Donald snapped.

"If you were to die today Donald, amazingly they would hide the truth from your eulogy also. What we are living is a lie man," Kem said. "Nobody will want to talk about how wicked we are in our eulogy, they will hide it with lies."

"Hold it, man, you are going too fast," Donald said. "Who says I am going to die?"

All the bullies laughed.

> A STAKE IS ON YOUR LIFE
> YOU DON'T KNOW THE TIME YOU DIE
> GAMBLE WITH TOMORROW
> AN ACCIDENT
> ANOTHER BET, ANOTHER TRY
> KNOW THE TIME IS BORROWED
> NEAR MISSES MANY TIMES
> GETTING OH SO CLOSE
> YOU REFUSE TO GIVE YOUR LIFE
>
> YOU'RE JUST ONE OF THOSE
> STANDING IN THE COLD
> PLAYING RUSSIAN ROULETTE
> WITH YOUR SOUL

Alex said laughing, "We all will. See what almost happened to Andrew!"

"I tell you, Anansi has infected you too Kem," Donald said, getting more impatient. "I am not going anywhere!"

"Tell Anansi I am not afraid of him," he continued defiantly.

"We are going to Anansi Donald," Alex said.

"You go but I am not coming," Donald said and walked away into the evening sun that failed to warm his cold heart.

> 1. THE HARDEST OF BULLIES HAS A HEART WHICH CRUMBLES UNDER THE HEAT OF GENUINE LOVE.
> 2. YOU CANNOT PLAN YOUR FUTURE OUTSIDE YOUR CURRENT ACTIONS. YOUR FUTURE LEANS UPON YOUR PRESENT ACTIONS FOR STRENGTH AND LOOKS TO IT FOR DIRECTION

ANANSI COUNSELS THE BULLIES

The following, day the group of bullies from Donald's gang boarded a bus to meet with Anansi. It was six of them. Alex, Andy and Bill were present. Donald was absent from the group. He was resolute.

The music on the bus played as they travelled. The song being played was Change.

The bus driver pulled the bus to a stop in Anansi's neighborhood and said, "Nansie stop!"

Anansi was so popular that they called the stop after him, not the name of the street.

The bullies disembarked the bus.

As they walked up to the home of Anansi, Alex asked, "Do you think Anansi will be mad at us, knowing who we are and all?"

"He is not like that at all," Kem said. "He is...he is so different."

They walked the rest of the way in silence.

The sun was already sinking in the afternoon sky when the group of bullies turned up on Anansi's doorstep.

The bullies' arrival contrasted the perfect backdrop of beautiful architecture and landscape and made an amazing picture.

Everyone in the group felt that the picture perfection of the surroundings could only be paralleled or even bettered by the time they were about to spend with Anansi himself. The sunshine had entered their hearts as they walked up the driveway. They already felt a radiation of warmth they could not explain. Kem leaned forward and knocked on the front door of Anansi.

The servant who answered the door recognized Kem immediately and said, "Hello Kem. It is

so very good to see you again."
"It is so good to be back," Kem said.
"I see you have brought your friends," the servant responded.
"Hello everyone," he said greeting the entire group with a warm smile, "Mr. Anansi is expecting you."
The servant brought them into the room popularly called the Anansi Room and said, "Please sit. Make yourselves comfortable. Mr. Anansi will be with you shortly."
The servant then pointed to a big computer screen with game controllers and said, "You may try the game; I will bring you some refreshments."
The servant then turned the screen on and stepped out.
The screen flashed and a demo of the game began to play with audible instructions.
"The object of this game is to escape the predator. You have a number of small creatures to choose from as your player."
The announcement ended.
Bill took the controls and said, "Me first. Watch me win!"
He selected a rabbit and aimed it in a run down a pathway to safety.
A big dog darted after the rabbit.
Bill did not expect this. He tried to move but got little response from the controls.
The dog pounced on the rabbit and the words, "Game Over!" came on the screen.
"My turn," Alex said.
"No man," Bill demanded, "I haven't got it yet."
"Ok but press that button on the controls to move," Alex said.
Bill pressed the button and started the game again.
The dog came darting at the rabbit immediately.
Bill set his rabbit running in a side lane to avoid the dog. The dog stopped and Bill celebrated.
He brought the rabbit out in the open heading for safety.

Just then an eagle came down.
Bill set the rabbit darting back. The dog who was waiting came and held the rabbit.
"Game over!" the audio on the game said.
Anansi, who was watching everything from behind an opaque screen door came into the room at that moment and said to everyone, "Hey guys." He then looked at Bill and said, "Bill, I see you are having fun.
"No fun at all, sir," Bill said. "These big guys hardly give me a chance to learn the game." He was referring to the dog and the eagle.
"So what do you think of them?" Anansi asked.
"They are really mean," Bill responded. "If there was just a way to let them know how frustrating it is for this little guy."
Anansi smiled to himself, "This is going just fine!"
"Imagine if it was not a game, and it was real life," Anansi said.
"We would find a way to get that eagle and that dog," Bill said. "We would teach them a lesson not to be mean."
"What if it was not a dog or an eagle, but it was real people making life difficult for other students to learn or to settle at school?" Anansi said.
"We would..." Bill started. Then stopped himself. He placed his hands on his mouth. The room was very silent.
Bill and all the other bullies looked down at the ground ashamed. They were afraid to look at Anansi. Anansi could see they got the message.
"You would...?" Anansi said, prompting Bill to finish his thoughts.
Alex responded instead, "Sir, we would...we would not have understood how frustrating and evil we were if you had not put it this way. We have been eagles and bulldogs to the weaker students."
Anansi said softly in a very gentle tone, "I know."
Anansi then turned on a large TV screen that filled up one of the walls. He then turned on a film

in 3D.

The bullies could see birds on an island. Something was wrong. The birds on the island were dying.

"We are dying, the water is poisoned," Crow said.

"What are we to do? There is just one bucket of drinking water left," Pigeon said.

"There is a cure but we must get it before the water is finished. If we put it in the bucket then pour the contents into the stream, it will be cured." Hawk said.

"I know," Pigeon said. "But it is all the way in the bird kingdom, and there is no way to get there and back in time."

"I just hope the king sees our plight and sends someone to save us soon," Parrot said.

Bird Kingdom was in the heights, a place named Rock. It was not visible to the birds. It was a beautiful place where eagles lived.

King Eagle and Prince Eagle ruled from their majestic heights with Prince Dove. The problem on Bird Island was caused by disobedience. They abused and corrupted the living water that flowed there. In the Bird Kingdom everything was perfect.

King Eagle said to Prince, "I am sending you down to Bird Island with the cure for the water. We cannot allow these birds to die. They came from us. They were disobedient, but we cannot forsake them.

You must keep this cure in your mouth for safety and only let it out to put it in the bucket of water. This is so important that I am not sending any of our servants. You have to do it yourself my son Prince. Remember you cannot be aggressive, no matter what happens. On Bird Island, you will be humble and pretend to be just as they are."

"I will go father," Prince said.

Prince Eagle always honored his father. He would go although he knew the journey could be dangerous.

The cure was placed in Prince's mouth and he set off.

After a long flight, Prince arrived at Bird Island. He attempted to go near the bucket of water to place the cure in.

Hawk who was also a big bird said, "What is it that this fellow thinks He is doing? Stop him!"

Everyone rushed to stop Prince.

They held on to him and pulled him away from the bucket. Prince did not exert his authority or his great strength. He wanted so much to tell them who he was but the cure was in his mouth and his mission was to place it in the bucket.

"So he wants a drink of water," Hawk said. "Here is some poison water."

He took a cup of poison water and threw it on Prince.

Prince tried to talk again but his mouth was full.

"Do not open your mouth or else," Ostrich said.

"Let us teach him a lesson so that no one will come and try this ever again," Hawk said.

"Let us nail him to that apple tree," Woodpecker said.

All the birds clapped and jeered.

Pigeon said to himself, "We are all dying from thirst and these birds have time to be so mean."

As they held Prince, Woodpecker nailed one wing to the tree and then the other.

Prince was strong, but he did nothing to save himself. King Eagle had commanded him not to exert his power and authority on Bird Island.

Prince felt the pain move through his entire body. He opened his mouth to scream and the cure fell out.

"What is that falling from his mouth?" Pigeon asked.

"It is the cure," Hawk said, looking sheepishly.

Crow said in that moment, "I recognize him now. It is Prince Eagle."

Prince Eagle sighed and lifted his head toward the birds then died.

Everyone wept and felt ashamed as they took up the cure.

They felt even guiltier for they knew the Prince had the power to destroy them and save himself, but he opted to die. They were amazed by the depth of his love and care for them.

The lights in the Anansi Room came back on. All the bullies felt sorrow at this sad and tragic movie. Bill and Andy had tears in their eyes.

Alex was angry. He said in anger, "He did nothing to deserve death. He was just trying to help!"

"This is what happens when we pick on a person without hearing their heart or knowing them," Anansi said.

"Do you remember John?" Anansi asked. They all nodded in acknowledgment. How could they not? The very question from Anansi tugged at their conscience like the rope of a boat being towed. "Look at him now," Anansi said. "He is such a blessing."

The bullies had no reply. They all nodded.

"Don't get angry with these birds," Anansi said as the light came on.

The television screen was replaced with a big mirror.

"See who the real bullies are," Anansi said as they stared at their own reflections in shame.

"I feel so awful and mean," Bill said, removing his mask before his colleagues.

The screen then shifted again to the television screen with a still picture of the birds looking guilty at Prince's dead body on the tree.

Anansi said to the group, fidgeting before him, "Jesus tells us to examine ourselves. Take the beam out of our own eyes before we pick on others."

A popular singer puts it this way, "Look, examine the man in the mirror. Speak to him to change his ways."

Anansi opened a big screen door to the garden. On the screen that blended into the garden the bird was pushing the bee away from a petal.

"That poor bird is rough," Anansi said, "but I am sorry for him."

Sorry?" Alex questioned.

"He lost his father early," Anansi said.

"His heart is good but the insecurity drives him to seek control."

The bullies blushed.

"Has any of you ever been without a father?" Anansi asked.

"Dad is there but he is never there," Alex said.

"I do not know my real father," Bill said.

"I grew up with my grandmother since I was six years old. She took me out of the children home after my parents went to prison." Andy said.

"I know someone who lost his father early." Anansi said. "Yet, he is so sweet and responsible. He found Jesus. Others have achieved greatness through discipline and good choices."

"You see, Andy, Bill, Alex, when you have a bad situation, it is no excuse. You can choose to make the world better for others or choose to make it difficult."

"We will make our world better," Bill said. And the others agreed.

"You can choose to be healed or to magnify your problems," Anansi continued.

"We want change," Andy said.

The servant brought refreshments, and they ate silently, almost in mournful reflection. "I invite you to be a part of my public forum on bullying on the weekend," Anansi said.

He intended to honor them and give them an opportunity to show everyone that they were sincere about changing.

Anansi gave all of them assignments and told them, "Study these characters and be ready to answer the question. I will have a reward for you then."

> Walking in the path of destruction
> Remove your foot from every evil way
> You will not fall into corruption
> He's building you like blocks every day

> Know that you are under construction
> And if you will do what He says
> Give your ears to His instructions
> Leaning on the Lord there is change

The bullies left looking very happy and reflective but resolute. The session was short but very productive. Most of all it gave them a way out.

> **IF YOU FIND YOURSELF IN THE WRONG PLACE, AMONG THE WRONG CROWD, DOING THE WRONG THINGS, YOU CAN RIGHT THE WRONG, GET OUT AND GET HELP!**

BOOK FOUR

ANANSI'S PUBLIC FORUM ON BULLYING

CHAPTERS IN BOOK 4

ANANSI PREPARES FOR THE BIG DAY

This was a big day for everyone. It was the day of Anansi's public forum. Today, he would address bullying.

All the students in the schools around were buzzing with excitement at the prospects of this Anansi event.

The parents wanted their children to attend. They were told everyone in some way was affected by bullying. Some people were affected directly, some indirectly and some were perpetrators.

"Anansi always had fun and give-aways at all his events, yet the message he delivered was always real and resonating," one child could be heard telling another.

"I want a good seat," the other child responded.

Donald, in the meantime, was meeting with some area gang members. They were led by a cousin of his.

"How hard do you want us to hit him Don?" Cruz, Donald's cousin asked.

He was a burly tattooed man in his mid-thirties who had been in and out of prison.

"Take him out completely," Donald responded. "He is mashing up my turf."

"We will take him immediately after the forum," Cruz said. "Don't you worry cousin, Anansi is finished."

"Thank you, Cruz. I know I can depend on you," Donald said and slipped away.

The auditorium was filled to capacity an hour before the forum started.

Anansi had given special instructions to the organizers, "The front row seats are reserved for bullies and children who are directly impacted by bullies."

The chief coordinator had responded, "We have coordinated with the guidance counselors and all the

children identified will be sitting on these reserved seats with their parents."
"Excellent," Anansi said.

Anansi had met with Deep, his interactive robot computer to research some of the most effective methods of dealing with bullies.
He had asked Deep, "Deep, how do you get bullies to stop bullying?"
Deep had responded in his usual rhythmic style.

"There is reactive and proactive aggression," Anansi recited as he meditated on his preparation for the evening.
"Proactive aggressors lack remorse for their hurtful behaviors. They can be expected to excuse their behavior by finding rational excuses for why aggression is justified."
"Proactive aggression can be expected to continue until proactive aggressors develop genuine empathy for others; until their aggressive behavior ceases to satisfy their evil appetite; or until they have access to more satisfying, pro-social ways to maintain positive self-esteem.
None of these counteracting conditions is likely to occur spontaneously and without intervention for several reasons. First, a concern for others is developed over time and by process a sense of conscience regulates them."

Deep had also said, "They will need the motivation to change because proactive aggression is an internalized, automatic behavior. Proactive aggressors are not likely to evaluate its harmful consequences as negative.
The best way to intervene is to get proactive aggressors to develop a level of empathy for others that effectively restricts their willingness to hurt others for personal gain.
Anansi, you will have to help them to acquire pro-social behavior and to prevent aggressive ones.
Empathy does not develop overnight. It occurs when caring for others is both modeled and valued at home by a child's parents or caregivers.

Anansi, empathy development, like all developmental change, occurs gradually over time, although, the necessity of stopping the aggressive behavior is immediate.
Bringing an immediate stop to proactive aggression will be a challenge for children who have chronic bullying behavior."

Anansi had processed all this information and prepared his session with all this in mind. Anansi used the words of a popular song to frame a prayer to God:

> HOLY SPIRIT LEAD THE WAY
> COME AND GUIDE MY HEART
> I WILL FOLLOW YOU WITH PRAISE
> TAKE ME WHERE YOU ARE
> LET THE HEAVENS NOW AWAKE
> AS I PRESS INTO YOU LORD
> HOLY SPIRIT LEAD THE WAY
> TAKE ME WHERE YOU ARE
>
> I'VE GOT THIS DESIRE
> DEEP DOWN IN MY SOUL
> TO KNOW YOU IN A WAY THAT
> NO ONE HAS KNOW YOU BEFORE
> LIKE THE PASSION THAT TOOK MOSES
> TILL YOU PLACED HIM IN THAT ROCK
> HOLY SPIRIT LEAD ME
> TO THE FULLNESS OF YOUR HEART

Anansi had also prayed, "Lord help me to meet the needs of all the people coming today. Amen."

Anansi arrived at the forum venue an hour before the starting time. He drove up in a carriage and entered the auditorium to the cheers and standing ovation of all the people in attendance.
"Lord, to You be all the glory and the honor," Anansi said in his heart. "I am just a fifty dollar note in Your hand."

Anansi hummed as he proceeded:

> A CURRENCY DON'T DICTATE
> HOW IT SHOULD BE USED
> THE ONE WHO SHOULD RECEIVE IT
> OR WHAT IT IS USED TO DO
> IT DOES NOT TELL ITS OWNER
> WHERE IT WANTS TO GO
> AND EVEN SO MY MASTER
> I SUBMIT MYSELF TO YOU
>
> SPEND ME LIKE THE FIFTY DOLLAR NOTE
> LET ME BE THE ONE YOU USE THE MOST
> A CURRENCY OF HEAVEN
> TO BE SPENT DOWN HERE ON EARTH
> TO BE TENDERED BY THE PEOPLE
> USE ME LORD

Anansi took the time out to greet some individuals, especially those seated in the specially reserved areas. These were the bullies, their parents and persons being bullied.

Donald was seated in the front row in a special seat reserved for him. His mother was seated beside him.

When Anansi reached Donald, he extended a hand, leaned over, looked into his eyes and said, "Hello Donald. It is such a pleasure to have you. I am hoping you will be able to help us get the message out to everyone today."

"Ur...sir...," Donald stumbled. He did not know what to say. He felt a warm stirring inside. "This is not the Anansi I wanted to meet," he thought. "He is too warm and personal, too kind and loving. No wonder everyone loves him. Perhaps I was wrong to arrange his demise when he leaves this forum."

"Can I depend on you?" Anansi continued in a warm tender voice.

Donald growled as if to fight back the warm unusual feeling inside. He needed to focus. "This has to be about my turf only!" he said to himself.

He looked at his mother and knew she expected him to cooperate so he nodded.
Anansi disappeared backstage as the music played softly, I HAVE MET LOVE.

THE INFORMATION YOU HAVE ABOUT YOURSELF WILL DETERMINE THE LIMIT YOU PLACE ON YOURSELF. DO NOT LET GOLIATH(A BULLY) BE THE ONE TO TELL YOU WHO YOU ARE OR WHAT YOU CAN DO.

LESSONS FROM AN INTERACTIVE RAP

The starting time had come. For the many passionate students waiting in anticipation, it was too long. At exactly 1:00 pm, the music died and the curtains of the stage were drawn.

On stage, was a cast of about twenty students from various schools and they were dancing to the song, CHANGE.

This presentation was very spectacular as it featured the dancers changing clothes and appearing miraculously in front of the audience.

There was a drama line included in the dance performance that featured various individuals at the crossroads making life impacting decisions. Some changed for the better, some for the worse based on the decision they made.

The dance mime ended with a thunderous applause from the audience.

The message was very clear: Change is possible but it is not automatic, it is based on positive choices.

Anansi came on stage immediately to the song, FIFTY DOLLAR NOTE, his theme song, and the people stood, clapped and danced.

> SPEND ME LIKE THE FIFTY DOLLAR NOTE
> LET ME BE THE ONE YOU USE THE MOST
> A CURRENCY OF HEAVEN
> TO BE SPENT DOWN HERE ON EARTH
> TO BE TENDERED BY THE PEOPLE
> USE ME LORD

The volume of the song lowered and Anansi's voice came through the microphone he was wearing,

"Thank you all for coming. This is our forum on bullying. We love bullies, we don't like what they do, but we love them.

For everyone who came here with the title, bully, I am believing that after this forum no one will consider you a bully anymore.

We begin with a dance off.

Those students at Champion School who knew John may not have known he is a very, very good dancer."

There was a loud applause from the audience but especially from Champion School. Some were shouting, "Go John!"

"John is going to come and dance to this Anansi Rap. I am going to invite three persons to come and face off with John. You must be on the front row to participate in this. The winner gets to participate in the money grab.

Now, can I see the hands of all the dancers?" Anansi said to a rhythmic rap beat.

Hands went up all over the auditorium. "Remember," Anansi said, "you must be on the front seat to participate in this one."

There were a few hands up in the front seats and Anansi chose two of the notorious bullies he had heard about. "We have Howard, from James High and Raynard from Mayfield School.

Now, who will be the third person?" Anansi looked at Donald but he looked away. "I will leave Donald, for now," Anansi said to himself smiling.

Anansi selected Richard who had his hand up.

The three persons selected came to the stage and took their places beside John. They warmed up to the song Roulette.

It had a fast paced hip-hop beat but a gripping message.

> A stake is on your life
> You don't know the time you die
> Gamble with tomorrow
> An accident

Another bet, another try
Know the time is borrowed
Near misses many times
Getting Oh so close
You refuse to give your life

You're just one of those
Standing in the cold
Playing Russian roulette
With your soul

Know the time is borrowed
Near misses many times
Getting Oh so close
You refuse to give your life
You're just one of those
Standing in the cold
Playing Russian roulette
With your soul

Anansi said, "This is the rule.
Your dance must be clean, and creative but when
the music stops you must freeze in one place until it
starts again."
Anansi went to the side of the stage and began to
rap,

This is the story of David and Goliath
David was a boy, Goliath was a champion
Big and burly a monster of a giant
He thought David was easy
He did not know that

David had the truth
They can't bully you
When you have the truth
You won't bully too
If they know the truth

The music stopped and the dancers froze. Richard
had forgotten the rule and was moving around. He

then realized his infraction when everyone started laughing and froze.

While the dancers froze, a little girl pointed to the big screen that covered the entire wall behind the dancers. "Look," she said, "there is a big burly man, full of muscles on the screen."

"He must be Goliath," an adult sitting beside her said. "Yes, and he is moving towards a small man… no, he is not a man, he is just a little more than a youth. That must be David, mother," she continued. "And look," she said excitedly, "he has his sling in his hand."

"We are about to witness something tremendous here today," her mother said.

As Goliath advanced, the screen froze, and Anansi continued his rap.

As Anansi continued to rap the dancers moved into action.

Anansi rapped,
>A bully will shout to make you afraid
>To frighten you, to intimidate
>Stand up strong like you own the world
>Speak back to them with the holy word

>David had the truth
>They can't bully you
>When you have the truth
>This is the truth
>You won't bully too
>If you know the truth

The rap paused. The dancers froze.
The screen flashed
>Goliath was shouting and all the people of Israel were running away.

David came and said, "Who is this uncircumcised Philistine to defy the people of God whom He chose, His special creation?

You come to me with sword and shield, but I come in the name of the Lord. I am going to kill you and

cut off your head and feed you to the vultures."
"Ah, David is running at him," the audience gasped.
Goliath looked visibly surprised and amazed that this little boy was running at him.

The rap restarted:
      You've got to stand up
      Stand up for your rights
      You are a perfect creation in Christ
      Let no one judge you by your:
      Height, your size, the way you look
      Or what you have
      By the cover of the book
      For what you have inside is real
      One giant down, the true Giant is seen

      David had the truth
      They can't bully you
      When you have the truth
      This is the truth
      You won't bully too
      If you know the truth
      Inside you may be hurting and bruised

The rap paused. The dancers froze.
On the big screen, David's hands were up in the air celebrating. The sword of the giant was in his hand and his foot was on the giant's body.

Anansi restarted his rap:
      Goliath saw a boy who was easy meal
      God saw a king who would be champion for Him
      The bully saw himself as too big to beat
      David saw the bully as too big to miss
      God saw the bully as too small to be significant

      David had the truth
      They can't bully you
      When you have the truth

This is the truth
You won't bully too
If you know the truth
Inside you may be hurting and bruised

Anansi then said to everyone, "Do you have a winner for our dance off?"
A loud chant went up from Champion School and was quickly joined by everyone else, "John, John, John!"
"We have a winner," Anansi said. "Let us hear it for John. John had some amazing moves didn't he?"
The audience applauded in agreement.
   "John will get an automatic place in the money grab," Anansi said. "The others will get to join John if they can tell us three things they learnt from the rap and the movie clips."

Just then a glass cubicle filled with fifty dollar notes was unveiled.
   "You will get to go in to grab and to keep all you can grab," Anansi said.
Donald's eyes lit up with immediate interest and Anansi took note.

The song Fifty Dollar Note began to play:
   Use me like a fifty dollar note
   Let me be the one you use the most
   A currency of heaven
   To be spent down here on earth
   To be tendered for your people
   Use me Lord

At Anansi's invitation, Howard stepped up. "What have you learnt Howard?" Anansi said applauding him.
Howard said:
   1. A bully will always try to intimidate you and make you afraid. If you run away they win.
   2. When a person shouts at you and bullies you, you can stand up to them.

3. If you know the truth of who you are, no one will be able to bully you.

There was a continuous wave of applause from the audience at Howard's excellent responses.
The applause was sustained and continued even after Raynard started his response:

1. Your height or size or the way you look is just like the plain cover of a beautiful book. It does not tell the true story. It does not truly reflect who you really are.
2. If we embrace who we are in God, we will not bully and we won't be afraid to stand up to bullies, just as with David.
3. How God views a situation is what it really is. How God views you is who you really are.

The audience applauded him appreciating his answer also.

Richard was the last up. He had shouts of encouragement from the children of Champion School as he said,

1 Don't let your size or physical incapacity prevent you from dreaming big.
2 Fear fuels bullying, confidence upstages them. Your confidence should be based on the truth about yourself. The truth about yourself is found in God.
3 Bullies make themselves bigger than they really are. Everyone who makes themselves too big is very small in the eyes of God. Those who humble themselves are big in the eyes of God. He exalts them.

When Richard finished, there was a rousing applause for all the participants and for their insightful and powerful answers. Everyone shouted "Yeah, yeah," to encourage him and applauded.
Each school seemed determined to acknowl-

edge the amazing insight being shared by some of their toughest bullies. They stood up and applauded delightedly.

Richard kept his eyes away from Donald, his former gang leader, all the time he spoke. When the applause started, however, and when the entire auditorium stood up in acknowledgment, Richard looked directly at Donald. For the first time, he saw a sign of weakness. Donald looked away.

"Please cheer them on as they grab," Anansi said. "The moment the participant enters the cubicle, the money will begin blowing all around them. They have three minutes to grab all they can. You are first up John."

The applause restarted as John entered. John entered and began grabbing and stuffing his pocket. It was difficult since the money was blowing everywhere.

Everyone was cheering him on and some were laughing as he let go of a hand full of notes to grab another.

By the time he devised a plan and was able to stuff notes in his pocket he had $2,250.00.

The other three followed to the continuous applause and laughter. Raynard grabbed the most money in his short time. He had $3,850.00.

The audience applauded them. Some envied them and hoped they would get a chance to grab also.

Anansi ushered them off stage then and said, "I need four other persons from the audience to come and grab. Anyone can try, if you can tell me what this Anansi Quote means, you are in:
'Never destroy a tree to get to the forest.'"

The hands started going up immediately. Anansi had workers all over whose responsibility was to listen to the answers of the participants and filter them to save time.

Four persons were selected and sent to Anansi.

The first person who came was Elle. She was from

Sunset High School.

Anansi looked at her gently and said, "So you have an answer, Elle."

"I do," Elle replied, "When the trees are destroyed, there will be no forest, the trees collectively comprise the forest. You cannot destroy people to gain love."

"That was exceptional!" Anansi said, dragging the "ex" and lowering his voice showing great respect. The applause from the audience was thunderous.

Anansi invited the other three participants to quickly say their points and go and grab. The first one came and said,

"I am Raynor. You will lose everything you seek to achieve when you bully.

Bullying breaks down the foundations of respect in order to gain respect. Very soon, bullies will realize their forest has no trees."

"Awesome," Anansi said as the applause exploded. It was obvious his ushers had done an excellent job in filtering the responses.

As Raynor went to grab, Wayne came forward.

"Bullying is counterproductive. It is like tearing down the roof above your head"

The audience applauded in appreciation.

Janet was last up. She said, "The gains from bullying are not lasting. Bullies create more damage to themselves and others in the long term. What they seek is not what they get. It pleases a bully to cut down a tree, or an individual, but they are unable to see the trees that are missing and absent from their forest until they are alone or in jail."

The applause continued throughout. All the answers were exceptional. Anansi was amazed.

As they grabbed for cash Anansi said, "This next session will be conducted by my robo-computer, Deep."

EMOTIONAL BULLYING ADDRESSED

Deep was a spectacle as he marched in on six legs rocking to the song Fifty Dollar note!
The auditorium erupted with laughter.
The computer like face with mouth and nose was enthralling.
Everyone leaned forward to have a closer look.
Donald too was on the edge of his seat.
The auditorium erupted with laughter as Deep mimicked Anansi's voice and said, "Anansi, Anansi, Anansi! This is me, I live this song."
Anansi too was laughing. "No doubt my theme song," he said, "Fifty Dollar Note."
"I will introduce a topic," Anansi said. "You may ask Deep any question on the topic, and he will answer you.
If you want to ask a question, please put your hand in the air and the ushers will escort you to a microphone.
I want to talk about Proactive Aggressors.
Not the ones that we recognize every day, the visible bullies. I want to talk about the deceptive ones, some of whom are probably sitting here today unknown. I want to talk about emotional bullies, frenemies.
There are bullies sitting among us today who do very evil things but pretend to be innocent, to be angels.
There are some sitting among us here who have been bullied, who are hurting, but you cannot tell your story. Nobody believes you."

The MC selected a track and played softly as Anansi continued.

> Love will pick you out on the globe
> Among the millions with you, it finds your soul
> It will amaze you how straight it goes
> And anywhere you are around the world

"If you have been bullied in this way, you will get a chance to tell your story but you cannot call names," Anansi continued.
"Deep, tell us, how do we define an emotional bully?"

Deep spoke in his semi-mechanical voice:
"Some bullies use force to gain control. Emotional bullies are bullies who do not have the physical advantage. Instead, they turn to deception, coercion and manipulation to gain the control they need for a positive self-image.
They use rationality, logic, verbal proficiency and emotional control as their means of bullying. They calculate and patronize to gain an advantage."
"Thank you Deep," Anansi said.
"Do we have any questions for Deep?"
The hands started going up all around the auditorium. The ushers could be seen moving around. One person was sent to a nearby microphone and she said,
"My name is Anna. I have had that experience. Everything I say gets twisted. The girl is very popular and no one believes me. Why do people do this?"
Deep showed a mechanical face of concern that made everyone laugh. It then responded with the most serious answer.
"Why do people do this?
It may not be plain but they do this to gain
Status, dominance and control
They lack empathy, so to bully for them
Is pleasure and satisfaction
Control for them is a pressing and sadistic need,
So it does not matter how they make others feel
They do what they do without feelings or care
They need worth, and they step on others
to get there

They play games, but you play life
For them, the two are just alike."
The applause was thunderous.
Another girl came up.
"My name is Angel. Deep, why does no one believe us?"
Deep responded:
"So why does no one believe an angel?"
Everyone laughed.
"Emotional bullies are like the serpent in the garden
Cunning, calculated and crafty even
They will not be direct but push sensitive buttons
To get an emotional response to label you
They cry tears to pretend, but it is just a show
Then laugh the next minute after they
deliver the blow
They calculate and know when the time is right
To do their evil out of sight
And they get involved and volunteer
To be the perfect devils in angels' wear."
The audience applauded.
"Frenemies and emotional bullies pretend to be perfect to everyone," Anansi said as Deep concluded, "while they secretly torment their victims."
Another girl came to the microphone:
"My name is Marcia. I can relate to everything you say.
"They always say exactly what people want to hear." She looked back at another girl who seemed to cringe.
"Please," Anansi said, "Try not to pick out anyone."
Deep nodded its head, and everyone laughed.
"You've just picked out many persons indirectly
with your statement," Deep said.
"Disingenuous is the word
They will say exactly what you want to hear
They open the door for their aggression
to continue without intervention from there
They display false emotions and shed

many false tears;
Eloquent in defending themselves so
it makes them appear
Powerful and ominous in the eyes of
their victims and peers.
They manipulate others' emotions
in their drive for personal gain.
Pressing sensitive buttons to prompt
emotional responses to justify insane
They do everything to win the trust
of those they see
who would be most likely to suspect
and intervene.
A proactive aggressor may seem to be
Two different persons effortlessly
One person in the eyes of authorities
And another in the eyes of their victims
from what they pretend to be.
A devil disguised as an angel of light,
They know with whom to pick their fight.
The weak, the isolated with no support.
But as the common saying goes
To see me and know me, are two different
persons in the same shoe."

The audience applauded.

"How do we get adults to believe us?" another asked.

"I will answer this," Anansi said.

"Teachers, parents, adults you must listen. Listen to the child. Never judge the truth by what you see or hear. Investigate, reserve your judgment and test the facts. Never prejudge a situation. Never take sides or be partial. That is ungodly, God is not partial in judgment. He has no respect for persons or personalities. He respects truth.

When you pre-judge, you risk harming the people you love. When you prejudge you protect bullies who are destroying themselves. When you prejudge you also push away those who are being harmed and expose them to emotional damage.

If you are a Christian, pray. Seek the wisdom of God

and His discernment.

You do not really know a person until you know a person. You do not really know a situation until the Holy Spirit reveals it; the one who knows every situation through and through.

Also do not be afraid to question the bully...ah...I mean your angel. There are ways to ask questions that are smart and revealing without being too distrusting or intrusive. You may just discover the lack of a foundational basis and the lack of empathy."

Anansi then turned to Deep. "Thank you for this wonderful insight Deep."

There was a thunderous applause for Deep as the mechanical computer bowed, or pretended to. Everyone applauded.

"Do you have anything to add Deep?" Anansi asked.

"Yes I do," Deep said. "Adults and caregivers, you must all learn to love, truly love.

L = Listen

O = Oust all bias and partiality

V = Ventilate the situation

E = Envelope and embrace the truth

Parents, affirm your children. The real or perceived absence of affirmation from significant others, parents, in particular, is the main reason they are emotional bullies. These children have come to derive a sense of self-reliance from their ability to succeed without and often do so at the expense of others. They normally display internalized resentment and anger over frustrated needs for security, and they keep others far enough away to protect their desired autonomy and self-sufficiency."

The audience erupted in applause.

"Well," Anansi said, "if we have so many persons here who have been bullied emotionally, it means we must have bullies here who have bullied others emotionally.

This is a moment like no other where bullies are not afraid to seek change and find freedom. You are not alone."

The song Change played:

> CHANGE, CHANGE
> YOU CAN HAVE IT IF YOU WANT IT
> CHANGE, CHANGE
> HERE IS A TREASURE YOU CAN GRAB IT
> CHANGE, CHANGE
> YOUR EVIL WAYS, YOUR DIRTY HABITS
>
> WALKING IN THE PATH OF DESTRUCTION
> REMOVE YOUR FOOT FROM EVERY EVIL WAY
> YOU WILL NOT FALL INTO CORRUPTION
> HE'S BUILDING YOU LIKE BLOCKS EVERYDAY
> KNOW THAT YOU ARE UNDER CONSTRUCTION
> IF YOU WILL DO WHAT HE SAYS
> GIVE YOUR EARS TO HIS INSTRUCTION
> LEANING ON THE LORD THERE IS CHANGE
> CHANGE

Anansi continued, "Emotional bullies are usually very good liars and deceivers. The Bible says, however, that lying is not good. Living a lie is very terrible. The Bible also says all liars will have their part in the lake burning with fire. It also says lying lips are an abomination to God.

If you are here, and you know you have practiced emotional bullying, you have smartly abused another person; you have deceived, and manipulated, be an Anansi Hero and stand up. Make a commitment to change. Anansi can help you.
It will take courage to stand, great courage and that makes you a real hero.

For everyone who stands, I will give an Anansi Hero pen. These pens are very exclusive, made with real gold, and you will be the only ones to own them. They signify that you had the courage to come out of hiding and to face up to the truth. It signifies your commitment to writing a new chapter in your life. It also gives you exclusive three-month access to the Anansi Hero's Club. It is an exciting club where you will have fun, and I will help you to get back on track.

One person stood, then two, then more, many more. Tears began to fall from the eyes of those children who were bullied but were never believed before.

Tears began to fall from parents, guardians, and other adults who never would have accepted the truth about their saints now standing exposed before them.

"Why did I not believe her?" one parent whispered.

"Oh no!" a mother said as her daughter stood, refusing to look in her direction.

"Thank You Lord!" some victims sighed. The responses were varied, powerful, and overwhelming. There was a thunderous applause from everyone else, and it encouraged others to stand.

The atmosphere was very emotional and celebratory. The only thing absent was condemnation. Anansi did not give it any invitation or room for it to feel welcome.

The song CHANGE played as the ushers brought Anansi Hero pens to everyone standing.

1. IF SOMEONE MUST FALL FOR YOU TO RISE, WHEN THEY RISE YOU WILL FALL.

2. YOU MAY LIVE BELIEVING THAT THE TRUTH IS WHAT YOU MAKE IT, THOUGH OTHERS BELIEVE YOU, YOU HAVE BOUGHT A LIE, AND THE DEVIL WILL HAVE SOLD IT AND BOUGHT YOU.

3. YOU ARE ON RECORD IN HEAVEN! NO NOT A QUESTION BUT A FACT; WHAT ARE YOU WRITING ON YOUR RECORD TODAY?

THE BULLIES REVEAL HOW BULLIES THINK

Anansi waited until the atmosphere settled down. Then he said.

"There are other proactive aggressors here. They are the ones we know as bullies. They are less discreet and very blatant with their actions. Everything that applies to emotional bullies applies to this other type of proactive aggression, except, one is disguised and one is done openly.

Those who are physically large and powerful will achieve that dominance through threats or acts of physical intimidation.

We are about to give fifteen automatic answer consoles to bullies from the different schools.

In this section, we will be asking some questions and those with the answer console will press Yes or No. No one will know who answered what. To-day, we will learn more about how bullies think and what motivates them from the bullies themselves."

Deep will compile the answers immediately. The ushers went around and gave Donald and fourteen other bullies answer consoles.

Anansi then read the questions as they came up on the big screen.

"Question1: Do you feel compelled to be a bully to gain status, control, self-confirmation, or just to feel gratified?"

There were fifteen responses of Yes. "One hundred percent Yes," Deep said in his deep computer voice.

"Question 2: Are you first attacked or provoked by the persons you bully?"

There were fifteen responses of No. "One hundred percent, No. No provocation needed." Deep said.

"Question 3: Who are your victims? Do you normally target the weak, the most vulnerable, the isolated and those who are least threatening?"
The bullies all continued to respond honestly, drawn in to the magical feeling and the honesty of the forum.
"One hundred percent Yes," Deep reported.

"Question 4: Do you feel remorse, sorrow or any form of empathy for your victims?"
The responses were swift, "One hundred percent, No. No empathy." Deep said.
One of the bullies commented under his breath, "How could we bully if we had empathy. I have never questioned my motive before now. Anansi is awakening feelings in me, now that I can see how others feel."

Anansi continued, "Question 5: Do you often develop good reasons to justify and excuse your behavior? Do you often convince yourselves and others why aggression was justified and unavoidable, even when you know it is not true?"
"One hundred percent Yes," Deep reported.

"Question 6: Do you often tell yourself that the measures taken by authorities to deal with your aggressive actions were unjust even when you know they were justified?"
The bullies all pressed the buzzer one more time, all conceding again.
This experience was very humbling for them but they knew they needed honesty to gain the freedom they now desired. They could see what they had pushed away before, the truth. "My behavior stinks," one bully was overheard whispering.

"One last question," Anansi said. "How would you like the opportunity to reverse your answers? Do you desire change?"
"Fourteen out of fifteen," Deep said to the thunderous applause of the auditorium. One person had abstained. Donald was still struggling inside.
He had arranged for his friends from an adult gang to shoot Anansi at the end of the session. Anansi

was a threat to them all and to their way of life. Now, Donald was bothered inside. This meeting with Anansi had forced him to listen to his conscience. He felt bad about everything.

"So now you know how bullies think," Anansi said, addressing the audience.
"A bully's life is just like a deforested reserve. They have cut down the tree of love and replaced it with anger and hatred. They have cut down the tree of empathy and replaced it with aggression. They have cut down the tree of remorse and replaced it with excuses and self-justification."

Deep recited a poem at this point:
"Why is there no love?
They have cut down that tree
Why is there no empathy?
They have cut down that tree
Why is there no remorse?
They excuse themselves
By making excuses to themselves
Refusing to face the truth themselves
And to hold themselves responsible."

"We are about to break for refreshments," Anansi said, "but before we do. I am going to ask everyone in this forum to take a big step. Let me see the hand of everyone, adults and children who promise me to participate."
It appeared that every hand in the auditorium went up.
"I want you to get up." Everyone stood up.
"While the song LOVE WILL PICK YOU OUT plays, find a person who has hurt you, really hurt you. Include the person who has hurt you most if they are here and hug them. Give them a big genuine hug."
Children were hugging bullies. Bullies were hugging parents and teachers. Children were hugging children. Husbands and wives were hugging. Adults were hugging adults. Tears were flowing down many faces yet there was such a sense of

relief and overriding satisfaction. Confetti was falling from the ceiling as the lights flashed.

One victim of bullying described it afterward, "This was heavenly. It was worth coming for."

"There are plenty of refreshments for everyone," Anansi said. "Pastries, fruits, nuts, snacks, juice. We come back together in thirty minutes."

1. *YOUR PAST FAILURES AND EXPERIENCES DO NOT EXCUSE YOUR PRESENT ACTIONS, IT ONLY VALIDATES THE CALL TO GREATER DISCIPLINE AND SACRIFICE.*

2. *IF YOU HAVE BEEN LET UP, OR LET DOWN, IT IS POSSIBLY JUST A SET UP FOR YOUR FUTURE, DON'T SIT DOWN.*

3. *BABIES CRY AND WHIMPER, BULLIES GIVE TROUBLE, WHAT IS A COMMON FACTOR? THE ABSENCE OF MATURITY; GROW!*

EMPATHY IN EVERYONE

The session resumed to the beautiful sound of Fifty Dollar Note. This had become a very special song to Anansi. It was a song that wrote his life story. It was a song that reflected his personal mandate and commitment.

Anansi danced gently to this song as the audience quickly regained their seats.

Without introduction, a motion picture came up on the big screen in 3D. Everyone was caught up in a rescue mission occurring at a beautiful lake. A boy who was dressed like an aristocrat had wandered into the lake and was in difficulty. The adults who were there with him had not seen what was happening.

Two men who were standing on the roadside saw what was happening.

The younger man spoke to the elder, "We are poor and they will kill us if we enter that property but we must do something."

The older man said, "I want to save that young mister, but I am not going over there. The security would be on us even before we get to the boy."

"We cannot just let him drown," the younger man said. "Let us shout and get their attention."

They began pointing and shouting frantically. "Help! The boy! Look, he is drowning!"

The couple at the lake side looked at them and looked away. The man with the woman said, "So if you are drowning then drown. We do not associate with people like you. Do not even look at us. Honey, do not even turn in their direction." As the audience watched aghast, the boy went under the water. "I am not waiting any longer," the younger man said. "I don't care what happens." He jumped the fence and chased for the lake in a dash.

The man at the side of the lake jumped into action immediately screaming, "Security!"

A security guard came running to tackle the intruder. The young man evaded him. He came again to tackle him, and he pushed him away. The entire auditorium held their breaths and pointed, hoping these people would see the danger. Hoping they would see the good this young man was attempting.

The young man reached the lake side and dived in. He pulled the boy from under the water. He had just gone down a second time.

He brought him to the shore and all attention was on the boy as they tried to revive him. The auditorium held their breaths until the boy began coughing. The man hugged the boy and the woman took over, showering him with hugs and affection as if he had been away for a long time.

The father looked at the security and turning to the young man he said, "Arrest this man!"

The audience gasped. Almost everyone screamed, "No! Oh no!"

The woman understood the injustice about to take place but did nothing.

The screen was turned off.

The people in the auditorium were riled up. They were angry, upset and emotional. They could not believe what just took place. Tears were in the eyes of many as their hearts burned within them for the young man.

The voice of Anansi pierced the atmosphere of disbelief and amazement. He was the only one able to talk at that moment.

"Do you see how evil bullying and discrimination can be?" he said.

"The purpose of this film is to capture the reactions of you all as you watched this evil in living color. Do not get angry. What you saw was just a film although this type of injustice happens all around us every day. It happens every time someone is bullied for no reason. In a minute, we will be replaying some of the funny reactions."

The film restarted with the boy in the lake

drowning. One woman had risen from her seat screaming, "Idiots! Look. He is drowning." Her face was made up, angry, and very concerned. Everyone laughed to see the look of intensity and alarm on her face.

There were many other funny reactions that kept the audience laughing at themselves.

When the man said, "Arrest him!" Anansi focused on the reaction of the bullies. Donald stomped his feet in anger. There were tears in the eyes of three big bullies.

The reaction ranged between anger and remorse. And in many cases it was very funny.

Everyone laughed at seeing the bullies like this.

"You see," Anansi said. "We all do care. There is something inside everyone that cries for justice. There is something inside everyone that hates in-justice. There is something inside of all of us called empathy. That something is who we really are. We have to fight that something every day in order to be mean and to be a bully. Today you could not hold that something back."

The audience applauded Anansi's words.

Anansi continued.

"God loved us all so much, He gave His only Son to die. They bullied Him and killed Him although all He was trying to do was help them." The applause started again.

He died asking God, the King Eagle, to forgive them, to forgive us all.

Today, if you have been bullied ask God to forgive the bullies. Jesus not only died showing us how to love, but He lived teaching us to love. Love is our greatest weapon and our most valuable as-set. When someone mistreats you, it is because they have not been taught love. Love them, pray for them, do good to them as Jesus taught us. The Bible says that love will always win."

The screen flicked back on without warning and they were again in the middle of the 3D movie. The security guard handcuffed the young man and

was dragging him away.
Suddenly, the boy who was saved ran to him and held on to his feet crying. "Thank you for saving my life," he said. "I love you sir."
The woman could not resist anymore. "Release him," she said. "If it was not for this man our son would have been dead. How can you be so uncaring and insensitive Jack?" she screamed at her husband.
Jack looked at his son, his face rigid and emotionless. He saw the tears in his son's eyes and his face softened.
"What am I doing?" he asked himself. "If you had treated us the way we treated you, our son would have been dead. I am so sorry sir," he said with tears in his eyes. "Release him immediately," he commanded the guards.
He then went a step beyond and said, "Please come for dinner tomorrow with your family so we can thank you properly. I will send a carriage out for you."

The older man stood outside the fence watching. The ground was awash with his tears for he was unable to contain himself. He knew within his heart, he had missed a very important moment. It was firstly an opportunity to save a drowning boy. Secondly it was an opportunity to save a situation, to create change, and it was because he was unwilling to take the risk. He was afraid to get hurt.

As the young man left smiling, Jack's wife turned to him and said. "Jack, now, I can love you as never before. I have never seen this side of you. I always thought you were a... well, an ignorant bully!"
"I was," Jack said. "I am so sorry. All these people need is an opportunity. We are no better than they are. We have deliberately kept them down. This man has taught me how to love. I was about to lose everything before he came. Our son is everything to me. I will begin the process of healing and building the bridge between us."

The audience cheered and many were in tears as the movie ended. Some of the bullies were crying also.

"Let me see everyone who will make a commitment from this day to choose love instead of deploying aggression," Anansi said.
The hands of many bullies were in the air.
"This means even when you feel you need attention, you will attract love to you by loving. No one can really force love. You force hate. Others will hate you instead.

Now, for those who are being bullied, promise me you will love the bullies. Love always wins. Jesus says you heap coals of fire on a person's head when you do good to those who do bad things to you. You infect their conscience, and force them to acknowledge that empathy is real. Do the opposite of what they expect you to do just as Jesus did."
The hands went up again and stayed up for a while. Anansi knew he had his audience.

The song Encore blazed from the speakers.
> ENCORE, LORD DO IT AGAIN
>
> WANT MORE, OF YOUR REFRESHING RAIN
>
> I'M SURE, THAT WHEN I GIVE YOU PRAISE
>
> THE DOOR OF HEAVEN YOU OPEN
>
> UNCOVER THE WELLSPRINGS AND FOUNTAIN
>
> AND POUR THE BLESSINGS DOWN
>
> ENCORE
>
> ENCORE - CLIVE WARREN

Anansi allowed them to settle, then he said in a serious voice:
"Right now, we will deal with another type of bullying, sexual bullying, and sexual harassment."

> 1. NOT BECAUSE YOU HIDE IT MEANS YOU DON'T HAVE IT, CRACK THE CRUST AND THE LOVE IN YOU WILL POUR OUT.
> 2. YOU KNOW JUSTICE AND INJUSTICE, YET YOU ONLY RESPOND WHEN THE BREAKING NEWS SAYS: JUST IN... IN-JUST-TIS HITS CLOSE TO HOME

SEXUAL BULLYING ADDRESSED

The big screen flashed and a brand new gold Ferrari was driven slowly across the screen on the dusty road. It looked spanking. Just then, the picture changed and the car lot of a Ferrari dealer was shown. There were spanking cars of the same brand and one that looked exactly the same. "If you were given a choice of these two cars, the one you saw driving or the one on the lot," Anansi asked. "Which one would you select?"

"The one on the lot," everyone shouted.

"Why?" Anansi asked.

"That is obvious," Donald answered. "Because it is not yet driven."

"So true," Anansi said. "No one will seek a used car over a new car. Once a car is driven off the lot, it loses its status of being new immediately and loses at least 25% of its value.

Now if the car is stolen from the lot by someone who never paid the price to own it, they will use it in hiding, scrap it, or sell if for much less than it is worth.

You are all treasures on God's lot. Young ladies, do not allow anyone to take you for a casual drive.

Do not allow anyone to take you from your Father God's lot without the right price and the right commitment. You don't want to be abused, scrapped or sold out for less than nothing."

The audience applauded.

"Can three ladies tell me how you can get scrapped or depreciated as a young woman?"

"Giving your body away casually?" one young lady said. "Sex before marriage," another quipped. "Sexting," another said.

"All of the above," Anansi said. "This is the internet age where sex is available at a click. That which God hates is made to appear normal. Every phone is now equipped with a camera. It is very

foolish to send your body parts to others by text. What happens when the relationship gets sour, you are betrayed and bullied into illicit behaviors.
Boys bully and pressure girls by sending them sexual images and girls bully girls to come and join them for the ride off the lot, stolen rides, and pretend to be untouched."
Girls bully boys into lustful attraction by wearing revealing clothing. If you are beautiful, and you know you are beautiful, you do not need to undress to attract a male, just dress to suit your godly elegance."
The applause was thunderous.
"Yes, yes!" someone shouted.
        "When Adam and Eve sinned, they discovered they were naked. Although no other human was around, they sought a covering for themselves. They sought any means possible to cover their nakedness, even fig leaves.
God made a blood sacrifice and covered them then. Today people look for ways to get naked and yet, appear covered. They love sin.
It is ok to please God rather than people. It is ok to honor God with your bodies. It is ok to be virgins. It is ok to wait on God. It is ok to cover your bodies. Your beauty and attractiveness comes from inside."
The adults in the audience applauded with many of the students.
Anansi continued, "Look at the screen and tell me what is common in these four pictures."
        The big screen came alive with four photographs. The first was God slaying an animal to cover Adam. The second was Abraham with the word circumcised across the picture. The third was Moses offering up a burnt offering through his brother Aaron. The fourth was Jesus on the cross, blood pouring from His side.
        "Death," someone said.
"Yes," Anansi said, "but a little more."
"Blood," another person said, then added, "sacrifice."
"Yes," Anansi said. "The sacrifice of blood.

"Whenever God ordered a covenant that is sanctioned by heaven, blood was required to seal it. The writer of Hebrews stated that there is no covenant, testament, without the shedding of blood.

God placed the hymen in the female to signify the blood covenant of marriage."

Many in the audience drew their breath at this analogy. It was profound against the background of how casual virginity is taken in today's society.

"I want to surprise many of you in this twisted society and say, it is abnormal not to be a virgin at marriage," Anansi continued.

"Your virginity signifies to heaven your marriage covenant."

There was a thunderous applause from the audience. Many of the female students were looking out of place feeling guilty.

"Everyone here who is still pure please stand."

Many of the other female students stood.

"Beautiful," Anansi said. "If I may steal a line from Sonia. Sonia wave your hand."

Sonia waved and Anansi acknowledged her with a bow.

"If anyone tries to bully you about your stance for purity, tell them, 'Any day I want I can become like you, you can never ever become like me.'"

Everyone applauded.

"Now if you will make a covenant with Anansi to commit to purity until you get married keep standing, the others may be seated."

One young lady sat and quickly rose again when she realized no one else was sitting.

"This covenant is before God and is only necessary because society has been teaching and bullying you to do the opposite. Ushers, please bring the rings."

The ushers came forward bringing a box of gold rings.

"I am going to ask you to come forward in a line so I can personally put the ring of your promise on your fingers myself. No one is allowed to take it off but your husband when he replaces it. Wear it proudly."

When he had finished giving the rings, Anansi said, "Our God makes all things new. Everyone who is not pure but commits to abstinence from now on until marriage, please stand up."
Many other girls stood up. Sonia was surprised to see the girls who had been pressuring her at school standing. "The ushers will bring your commitment rings to you," Anansi said.

"Let me see the men in this place who will commit to honor God until marriage. Heaven wants to acknowledge you."
The boys were resistant. Only a few stood.
"Ladies, give it up for them."
All the girls applauded.
Many more boys stood.
Anansi said, "I see you, I see you. God sees you. Do not be afraid to stand up and show yourself strong."
Some other boys stood up and Anansi acknowledged them saying, "I will take the time to meet with you all personally, you may be seated."

Anansi's semi-intelligent robo-computer made its entrance at that point and Anansi said, "Give it up for my computer Deep."
Everyone applauded.
Deep mocked a bow and everyone laughed. It was funny.

---

1. *YOUR BODY IS GOD'S TEMPLE, YOU HAVE THE KEYS BUT YOU DON'T HAVE THE TITLE OR THE RIGHTS TO DO WITH IT AS YOU DESIRE. YOU WILL BE HELD ACCOUNTABLE.*
2. *THERE WILL BE MANY BUYERS BUT YOU MUST BE ABLE TO SAY PROUDLY, I DID NOT SELL OUT... MYSELF!*

THE FOUR G'S OF BULLYING BULLIES FROM THE BIBLE

"Deep is going to help us with this final session. It is very interactive.
First Deep, tell us, why do bullies bully?"

"I call this the three G's, Anansi," Deep said. People bully for:

Glory- They bully to obtain status. To boost their self esteem.

Gain – They bully for the reward. The things they are allowed to steal.

Game – They bully for the pleasure. Just for play. This is sadistic but they get the kicks in seeing others suffer."

"Thank you Deep," Anansi said. "When bullies bully, they tend to forget about the fourth G, the Big G, God. God will always give an answer to the actions of the bully. Forgetting the Big G always ends in disaster for the bully."

"Now," Anansi said. "We want to identify some bullies from the Bible. Deep will act out a character and you will guess who the Bible character is. You will raise your hand and tell me, first your name, then who the Bible character is, which of the three G's was their motivation and what did the Big G do. Everyone who gets the answer correct will get a very special Anansi watch. It is exclusive and made of genuine silver."

Everyone knew Anansi was rich, very rich. He acquired most of his wealth by outsmarting others. Since he got saved, he became so very generous. He took every word and promise of God about giving and loving very seriously. He tries to emulate Jesus Christ in every way. His mantra and theme song is, USE ME LIKE A FIFTY DOLLAR NOTE.

Anansi indicated to Deep to begin.

"Let them work harder," Deep said in an authoritative voice.

On the big screen projected from his computer mechanism there were some men and women working. They were being beaten to work.

They were crying, "Ahh, this is hard. How does he expect us to make bricks without straw?"

"Who is their God? I will not let them go," their king said.

The hands began to go up.

Deep pointed to the person with the first reaction he picked up. It was a boy. He stood up and said.

"My name is Henry. It was Pharaoh in Egypt. He bullied and enslaved the children of Israel because they were a minority, and they were strangers in his kingdom. His primary motivation was Gain. They built his cities for free. The Big G, God, sent plagues on him and on his people and eventually destroyed his army in the Red Sea."

Anansi applauded, and everyone else began to applaud.

An usher went over and delivered an Anansi watch in a package.

Anansi said to the auditorium, "Can you see Pharaoh taking away the lunch of the Israelites, stealing their money, extorting, and blackmailing them? This is what the bullies at school do. They take another person's labor for free."

Anansi indicated and Deep continued.

Deep projected on the screen a very tall and handsome man with a crown. He threw a spear at a small boy who was playing an instrument for him. The hands went up immediately.

Deep indicated and a small girl no older than ten years old stood up. "King Saul and David," she said. "My name is Esther. Saul bullied David for the Glory. God removed him from being king."

Anansi began to applaud and everyone followed.

"Saul bullied David because of his own insecurity,"

Anansi said. "He saw David as a threat to his own glory. It is just as it was in another book in the Bible with your name intelligent young lady, Esther. Haman bullied the uncle of Esther, Mordecai for the glory. Mordecai would not bow down to him. He built gallows for Mordecai. The Big G orchestrated it so that Haman himself was hanged on the gallows he built, and Mordecai took his position. We cannot ignore the Big G when we bully."

An usher brought a package over to Esther and she opened it, still standing. Every eye turned to her gift. The watch was beautiful.

Anansi indicated and Deep continued. There was an air of excitement and expectation in the place.

"Which one of you cowards will come and fight with me?"

A big muscular dog was on the screen beating his chest. An army of cats was below him and every one of them trembled and scattered.

A little kitten came out and said, "Though I walk through the Valley of the Shadow of Death, I will fear no evil. I will! Who is this oversized Philistine to defy God's people?"

As he said this, one of the bullies jumped up. He was very intelligent and had figured out the Bible scene although Deep had used an abstract illustration.

Deep acknowledged him.

"My name is Richard. It is the story of David and Goliath. I believe Goliath bullied because of all three G's."

Some of the other boys started laughing but Anansi said, "No! Let him explain."

Richard was confident as he continued, "He wanted the glory, to be feared and to be given the top honor of his people. He was in it for the Gain also, he would have been offered great reward for his leadership role in the victory. He was also in it for the Game. I believe he enjoyed what he did. The Big

G empowered the kitten to defeat him with a small stone."

"Excellent," Anansi said applauding and laughing at his humorous use of the kitten to represent David. Everyone applauded thunderously. The ushers brought his package to Richard.

And Anansi indicated to Deep to proceed.

Deep projected on the screen. "She will be mine," an Eagle said, spreading his majestic wings out over his palace. It was obvious he was king of the eagles. He looked at a female eagle cleaning herself in her nest and said, "Beautiful. She will be mine."

The scene shifted, "Her husband," King Eagle said. "He is one of my faithful servants but he must die in battle. Let him carry his own death warrant to his commander."

The hands went up. Deep selected a chubby boy who was seated to the back. "David and Uriah," he said. "My name is Bigga..."

"No!" Anansi interjected. "That is what they call you. What is your real name son?"

"My name is Joel," he said.

"Your name is beautiful, Joel," Anansi said, "do not allow others to label you based on how you look, where you live or other things that make them feel better than you. You may continue."

"Thank you, Mr. Anansi, sir," Joel said. "My name is Joel. It is David and Uriah. David was in it for the gain, Uriah's wife. The Big G rebuked David and when David repented He forgave him."

Anansi applauded, "You are so right. David became a sexual bully, abusing his position of authority to force a woman to defy and violate the laws of her nation and the laws of her God. For this one time, David ignored the Big G and His stipulations on sex and covenant." The audience applauded once more as an usher went over.

"This is what happens when you engage in sex before marriage. You ignore the covenants and commandments of the Big G, just like David. Even though David was forgiven, he was severely punished. Every sin and every act of bullying carries a consequence."

Anansi indicated and Deep continued.

A woman was on the screen. She had a crown on her head. She smiled and everyone bowed down and honored her. They kissed the ground she walked on.

When she was in private, her face was distorted in anger, "These people are still talking about their God. I will punish every one of them and make them pay." She stepped out and saw one of her officials and smiled sweetly to him, wiping the frown from her face in a smooth move and his heart melted.

"Go out and get some wicked men. Let them tell lies on my neighbor that he has blasphemed God and the king. Then let everyone stone him to death. No one must know I am behind this."

"Certainly, my queen," the official said. "You are like an angel to us, you can do no wrong."

The woman went in to her husband and said, "Do not worry about it anymore, it is settled. Your queen has it all worked out. The plot of land you desire is yours." At this, the hands began to go up.

"Jezebel," someone shouted. Deep ignored him and selected a girl from the center row.

"My name is Destiny. The woman is Jezebel, her husband is Ahab. She plotted and murdered Naboth and stole his land. She was in it for the Gain and the Glory, to demonstrate her total manipulative control. The Big G was offended and caused dogs to eat her flesh outside her window."

Anansi led the applause again.

"Welcome, to Jezebel, the queen of emotional abusers, the real frienemy. She protected her public reputation by plotting and scheming. Everyone considered her the queen of hearts but in secret, she was truly a wicked witch. She never showed her manipulation and scheming side publicly. In public, she pretended to be perfect. She lured everyone away from worshipping God to worshipping Satan, the prince of demons, Beelzebub, called Baal in those days. Every emotional abuser has the spirit of Jezebel. Manipulation is witchcraft."

"We will do a few of other quick ones. Go ahead and shout it out if you know the answer. A man was being thrown into a lion's den..."

"Daniel," they shouted.

"Yes," Anansi said. "They bullied him because of the gain and glory. The Big G delivered Daniel and the lions killed his bullies instead."

The firstborn babies were being killed. A man and a woman were running away to hide their baby. "Herod and Jesus," some said.

"Yes," Anansi said.

The screen flashed again. A man's head was being cut off. "No James!" some women agonized. The Pharisees were happy. "He has Peter!" John and the others said as they began to cry out to God.

"Herod and the apostles!" some said.

"Yes, Herod," Anansi said. "He did it for the game and for the glory. He wanted to please the people. They worshipped him as a god. The Big G inflicted him with a disease and worms struck him to death.

"We are out of time, but we could continue and tell you about Cain and Abel. Cain did it for the glory, to get God's recognition. God rejected him and drove him from His presence as a vagabond. We could tell you about many others. Shenecherib who surrounded Jerusalem and told Hezekiah, 'We destroyed many nations and their gods. Your God cannot help you. We will do to you just as we did to the other nations and their gods.'

He did it for the gain and glory. All his army woke up dead the next morning. He was killed by his own sons in the house of his god, broken and ashamed.

The Big G, God's response to bullies through-out the centuries is always the same. He hates their actions and punishes them.

If you are a bully, you are in bad company. You cannot ignore the Big G. He will punish you.

The Devil is the biggest bully ever. Anyone who steals, kills or destroys is demonstrating his character. Anyone who helps the weak, and wounded is demonstrating the character of Jesus who came to give life.

Anyone who lies and deceives is demonstrating the character of the Devil. Jesus calls Satan a liar from the beginning. He cannot speak the truth even if he tries. Anyone who speaks the truth and is transparent is demonstrating the character of Jesus. He says I am the way and I am the truth.

The Devil tempted Jesus and offered Him Gain, Glory and Game. Jesus refused everything he offered. The Big G was more important to Jesus than everything else: Gain, Glory and Game."

"Remember," Anansi said, "Jesus teaches us to 'Do to others what we would have them do to us.' I am sure no bully would like to be bullied. The greatest commandment of God is to love the Lord with all our hearts, our minds and our strength and to love each other as we love ourselves. I am sure no bully would treat themselves the way they treat others. When we bully, we ignore the Big G. He will take action against us. He is righteous, which means, He must judge bullies.

The beauty about Him is that if we repent, He is righteous also and is faithful to forgive us of our sins and remove our iniquities"

The song ROULETTE echoed through the microphone.

A STAKE IS ON YOUR LIFE
YOU DON'T KNOW THE TIME YOU DIE
GAMBLE WITH TOMORROW
AN ACCIDENT
ANOTHER BET, ANOTHER TRY
KNOW THE TIME IS BORROWED
NEAR MISSES MANY TIMES

Getting Oh so close
You refuse to give your life

You're just one of those
Standing in the cold
Playing Russian roulette
With your soul

Know the time is borrowed
Near misses many times
Getting Oh so close
You refuse to give your life
You're just one of those
Standing in the cold
Playing Russian roulette
With your soul

"Over to you Deep," Anansi said.
The screen flashed again and a man was seen, battered and bruised. A crown of thorns was on His head and the people were screaming, "Crucify Him. Crucify Him!"
The screen flickered off. Deep took a bow and was gone.
"That last clip you saw," Anansi said, "Was Jesus. He was bullied to death by the Pharisees, the council, by Pilate and by all the people He loved and served. Just like most people who are bullied, He did nothing to deserve His treatment. He was nailed to a cross, yet, He died saying, 'Father, forgive them'. He took the punishment of us all, every person who angers God by bullying. This means there is hope for every bully, we do not have to face the wrath of God ourselves if we accept Him.

The Bible says that because Jesus has been bullied Himself, He can help all the bullies and everyone who has been bullied. If you want Jesus to help you let me see your hands."
The hands went up everywhere led by Donald and the other hardened bullies.

The DJ selected the song Encore to fit the moment.

> ENCORE, LORD DO IT AGAIN
> WANT MORE, OF YOUR REFRESHING RAIN
> I'M SURE, THAT WHEN I GIVE YOU PRAISE
> THE DOOR OF HEAVEN YOU OPEN
> UNCOVER THE WELLSPRINGS AND FOUNTAIN
> AND POUR THE BLESSINGS DOWN
> ENCORE

"Father hear their hearts and help them," Anansi said. The ushers then went around and took the names and the schools of everyone with raised hands. Anansi wanted to arrange follow-up and a program in these schools linked to the local youth fellowships to help all those who had responded.

The song Fifty Dollar Note played as some packages were brought out.
Some were big and beautifully decorated. Others looked normal. One even had what appeared to be garbage sticking out.
"We are about to close," Anansi said. "I will give some of you the opportunity to take a package. There are ten packages. We will first select five persons from the front row. Donald, come up here." Donald was excited to be selected. Four others were selected among the hardened bullies.
They each selected a package. All the bullies went for the bigger packages. Donald was a little more reserved and did not want to appear too greedy before Anansi. He had gained a lot of respect for him in this short time he had met him. He did not want to be too stupid either. He selected a medium package; well wrapped.
One of the bullies began to open his package and Anansi indicated for him to wait.
Anansi then called five other persons from the audience.
"John come up here," he said. He then selected four other students he knew were marginalized.

You may now select," he said.

The other students went for the biggest of the packages remaining first. John went for the package with the garbage sticking out. He had the experience before. Everyone including Donald, all the bullies, and everyone in the audience laughed at John.

John smiled and Anansi smiled at him and winked. John knew he was about to have the final laugh and the wink of Anansi confirmed it.

Each of the students selected had a package. Anansi told them to stand up facing the audience. He then told the audience, "Don't you want to see what's inside the packages?"

"Yes!" they all responded.

Everyone ripped the wrapping away and opened their packages. The three biggest packages were the greatest surprises. The biggest one was filled with slimy garbage. The second one had one small sweet in the middle of a wad of newspaper. The third had a fifty dollar note.

Everyone laughed at the expression of the bullies when they saw what was in their package. Donald received an Anansi watch, and he was elated. The last five were the happiest. They received gold watches, money, and other valuable Anansi products.

Everyone stared in awe as they saw what John received. He received five thousand dollars in addition to a watch and one of everything the others had.

The bully who had received the garbage was visibly distraught. He knew it was his fault. He was greedy, and it backfired but he did not like being embarrassed.

Anansi reached over and placed his hand on his shoulders. This comforted him.

"This is not to embarrass anyone," Anansi said. "It is just to teach you a final lesson. What I did not tell you is that the persons with the first five packages also get the opportunity to participate in the money grab."

The face of the bullies brightened as everyone applauded.

As they all went back to their seats happily, Anansi said, "You see, it is not the wrapping that matters but what is inside the package. It neither matters how you look, where you live, how you speak, if you are fit, or sick, or have a big nose or a straight nose nor does it matter the color of your skin. What really matters is what is inside your package. Everyone went after the pretty wrapping, yes, they ripped the wrapping and the packages in pieces to get at what was inside, right?" The audience nodded in agreement looking amazed.

"You see, deep inside, we all know this truth, the only thing that matters is what is on the inside. Fill yourself up with Jesus. Study the Word of God. Get your education. Read, listen, love and no one can stop you. You will not be bullied, and you will not bully."

Everyone applauded.

Anansi continued, "You were all made in the image of God. He says you were made fearfully and wonderfully. He packaged you perfectly but your package is not you. The "you" inside is very beautiful. Do not ever be distracted by the package or you will miss out on what John received.

Choose your friends well. Choose people who are going where you are going and who, when you cannot go, will take you and put you through the roof to get you in the presence of Jesus, instead of bullying or abandoning you.

Parents, guardians and caregivers, you have a role to play in all this. Your children bully because they lack empathy. Their love has run cold. Empathy does not come overnight. It occurs when caring for others is both modeled and valued at home by a child's parents or caregivers. You have your job cut out."

Everyone applauded.

"Have a great day everyone!" Anansi said in parting. The applause was thunderous and continuous as

Anansi exited to the tune Fifty Dollar Note. Everyone was standing.

Fifty Dollar Note played in the speakers to his exit.

Spend me like the fifty dollar note
Let me be the one You use the most
A currency of heaven
To be spent down here on earth
To be tendered by the people
Use me Lord

When my work for You on earth is done
Pull me from the circulation
And let me be replaced
By another in my place
Raise them up this minute
Use them Lord

ANANSI SHOT

Anansi went backstage and slipped out the door.

He would go across to the display hall for a few minutes before leaving.

Donald caught a glimpse of his gang leader cousin from the corner of his eyes standing outside. A feeling of desperation came over him. He had arranged with them to kill Anansi. He was powerless. He could not stop them now. He dashed outside to the sound of a single gunshot. Donald saw Anansi falling to the ground and he screamed, "Nooooo! Jesus, O noooo!"

People were gathering and Donald stepped into a corner and began to cry, drained and subdued. He had not prayed for a long time but this time he had no one else to turn to. Donald cried out silently, "Jesus, save Anansi and I will serve You."

The blood was flowing from a wound in Anansi's neck. His eyes rolled. They could hear him say, "Forgive them Lord," in a weak and muffled tone. He was speaking through the blood in his mouth. He then went motionless. Everyone was crying. They could not believe this. The clouds in the sky were overcast, and they knew heaven felt their pain.

The police quickly cordoned off the area. The ambulance was on the scene shortly afterward. Donald's cousin was sitting in a police car in handcuffs. He was caught running away from the scene. Donald could not look at him, it the paramedics took their beloved Anansi away that evening. He was in a coma. The doctor on the scene was overheard saying, "He has just the faintest indication of life, but it is unlikely he will make it."

The parting words of the song Fifty Dollar Note echoed in the hearts of every person there as salt on the lips in the parched desert. It left them longing... longing for water, thirsty and longing for their hero who made the song FIFTY DOLLAR NOTE his life. This last verse resonated:

WHEN MY WORK FOR YOU ON EARTH IS DONE
PULL ME FROM THE CIRCULATION
AND LET ME BE REPLACED
BY ANOTHER IN MY PLACE
RAISE THEM UP THIS MINUTE
USE THEM LORD

The words of this mournful song of prayer echoed in the heavens as the day went to sleep, no one knowing if their hero, Anansi, would ever wake up with it another time.

WHEN THIS WEARY WARRIOR IS WOUNDED IN THE FIELD
LET THE ANGELS UP IN HEAVEN
OFFER PRAISES JUST FOR ME
AROUND THE THRONE OF GLORY
WHERE ONE DAY I WILL BE
FROM THE THRONE OF HEAVEN
SING FOR ME

FROM THE THRONE OF HEAVEN
SING FOR ME, SING FOR ME
FROM THE THRONE OF HEAVEN
SING FOR ME
SATURATE MY HEART,
WITH HEAVEN'S SYMPHONY

FROM THE THRONE OF HEAVEN
SING FOR ME

TEMPTATIONS, PERSECUTIONS,
OR ANYTHING I MEET
ON THIS JOURNEY FOR MY KING
AND I'VE DONE EVERYTHING IN ME
YOU WILL FIND ME STANDING
BUT MY REQUEST WILL BE
FROM THE THRONE OF HEAVEN
SING FOR ME

Will Anansi die?
Follow us to find out in the next series of Anansi
Christian Counselor where we address gangs,
drugs and violence.